Alchemy
of the Heart

Alchemy
of the Heart

How to Give and Receive More Love

Elizabeth Clare Prophet
AND
Patricia R. Spadaro

SUMMIT UNIVERSITY PRESS®

ALCHEMY OF THE HEART
How to Give and Receive More Love
by Elizabeth Clare Prophet and Patricia R. Spadaro
Copyright © 2000 by Summit University Press
All rights reserved

Library of Congress Catalog Number: 00-106111
ISBN: 0-922729-60-3

SUMMIT UNIVERSITY ❦ PRESS®

Summit University Press and ❦ are registered trademarks.

Printed in the United States of America
06 05 04 03 02 01   7 6 5 4 3 2

Contents

Note: Because gender-neutral language can be cumbersome and at times confusing, we have often used *he* and *him* to refer to God or the individual. These terms are for readability only and are not intended to exclude women or the feminine aspect of the Godhead. Likewise, our use of *God* or *Spirit* does not exclude other expressions for the Divine.

PART ONE

OPENING
the Heart

The highest and most perfect love begins
with your individual expression of the heart—
and we all play the song of the heart
a little differently.

Increasing Our Capacity to Love

The beautiful souls are they that are universal,
open, and ready for all things. —MONTAIGNE

One day, very early in the morning, midst streets full of the sleeping, homeless poor of India, Malcolm Muggeridge accompanied Mother Teresa to the Calcutta railway station to see her off.

"When the train began to move," he said, "and I walked away, I felt as though I were leaving behind me all the beauty and all the joy in the universe. Something of God's universal love has rubbed off on Mother Teresa."

Something of God's universal love had rubbed off on Muggeridge as well. For those who embody the living flame of love are transformers—they transform whatever they touch. In Muggeridge's case, the crusty and agnostic English journalist was utterly changed by his encounters with Mother Teresa, whom he first interviewed in the 1960s.

"To me," he wrote, "Mother Teresa represents, essentially, love in action.... In a dark time she is a burning and a shining light."[1]

No matter who you are, no matter what your calling, you too can be a transformer of love. You can touch another heart and many other hearts who are waiting just for you—souls who will respond only to the unique expression of your heart.

When you get right down to it, there is nothing more important than increasing our capacity to love. A disciple once asked Gautama Buddha, "Would it be true to say that a part of our training is for the development of love and compassion?" The Buddha replied, "No, it would not be true to say this. It would be true to say that the whole of our training is for the development of love and compassion."

The apostle John said essentially the same thing in his beautiful exposition on love: "This is the message that ye heard from the beginning, that we should love one another.... He that loveth not knoweth not God; for God is love." If God is love and we were made in the image and likeness of God, as both Genesis and the scriptures of the East tell us, then at our very core we too are love. God created the universe so that we—and he—could experience more of the wonders of that love.

That is why most, if not all, of the critical issues in our life revolve around the innate need to give love and to receive love. When we lament the lack of appreciation or respect or even self-esteem in our life, what we are really yearning for is love. When we feel compelled to take those tortuous twists and turns through the labyrinth of life, painful as they may be, it's because we're trying to recapture the experience of divine love that is native to our soul.

The labyrinth takes us over the high peaks and into the deep chasms of our own inner terrain. The landscape has been shaped by our karma—the consequences of the choices we have made in the past to love or not to love. Each time we come to a Y in the road, we again come face-to-face with the choice—to love or not to love, to open our heart and share our gifts or to shut down and pretend no one is home.

Since the journey is not always easy, at times we take the safer, lower road so we can catch our breath. And sometimes we never make it back to the high road. It's understandable. Maybe we were deeply hurt in this life or a past life and we don't want to open our hearts and be rejected again. Maybe we're angry with others or even with God for the loss of a loved one. Or maybe we feel guilty about our own shortcomings and have convinced ourselves that we don't deserve to be loved.

In some cases, we unconsciously wall ourselves off. We retreat into the castle of our heart and position layers upon layers of defenses around it so that no one will get too close to us and we won't get too close to anyone else. But these defenses keep us insulated from the very thing we crave—an intimate experience of giving and receiving love.

That's when the universe conspires to wake us up and get us back on the high road. My teacher and late husband, Mark L. Prophet, once said, "All experiences on earth are to teach us the meaning of love. All relationships on earth are to teach us the meaning of love. Everything that takes place for the education of the soul . . . is to teach it the meaning of love. Because love is the power that shakes the universe and sounds the one pure tone that gives to every man the freedom to embrace his own divine presence, his own divine plan."

If we can embrace this truth—that all our experiences are designed to teach us how to give and receive more love—then suddenly the circumstances of our life make sense. We are awakened to the need for a higher walk with love. And the journey into those deep chasms and over those high peaks becomes a sacred trek.

"Be patient toward all that is unsolved in your heart and try to love the questions themselves," Rainer Maria Rilke once said. "Live the questions now." What are some of the questions that we must live on our journey of heart mastery? Here are just a few:

> *You knock at the door of reality, shake your thought-wings, loosen your shoulders, and open.*
> —RUMI

How can I open my heart and freely share my love with others? How can I empower my heart so I can fulfill my reason for being and soothe those who are in pain? How can I heal my own heart from the pain of the past and expand my capacity to love? How can I give to others and still find time to nurture myself? How can I enter my heart to fan the inner fires of love? How can I become a living transformer of love?

The alchemy begins with heart perspective.

 Heart Perspective

"Where is the locality of truth?" "In the heart,"
said he, "for by the heart man knows truth."

—*BRIHAD ARANYAKA UPANISHAD*

Alchemists of old are best known for their
experiments to transform base metals
into gold. But many alchemists were also explorers
of the spirit whose experiments were aimed at
finding keys to spiritual transformation and eternal
life. They were attempting to transform the base
metals of their lower self into the gold of their
highest potential.

Alchemy is self-transformation, the kind of
change that is essential to spiritual growth. As Jela-
luddin Rumi, Persia's greatest mystical poet, writes,
"The *alchemy* of a changing life is the only truth."[2]

The master alchemist and adept Saint Germain teaches that the point of reality is the heart
and that the key to understanding the reality of any
situation is heart perspective. "Centered in your
heart," he says, "you can see all things as they are."

Heart perspective is consciously thinking, feeling, acting and breathing through the heart. What-

ever you do, even if it's serving someone a cup of tea, it can be an extension of your heart. Heart perspective will change the way you treat others, the way they treat you, and the way you treat yourself. Heart perspective invites honesty and breeds compassion.

A wise monk was once asked by his companions what they should do if they saw a fellow monk snoozing during prayer time. "Should we pinch him so he will stay awake?" they asked. The monk replied, "Actually, if I saw a brother sleeping, I would put his head on my knees and let him rest."[3] That's heart perspective.

When we have heart perspective, we are committed to keeping a warm, open place in our heart where someone who is in pain feels safe to enter. Heart perspective is that creative genius that looks for ways to inject love into every challenge. It inevitably finds a unique and higher solution to a knotty problem.

In his book *Legacy of the Heart,* Wayne Muller relates a Vietnamese folktale that shows how a change in perspective can turn a seemingly impossible situation into an opportunity to give and receive more love. "In hell, everyone is given an abundance of food, and then given chopsticks that are a yard long," writes Muller. "Each person has all the food they need, but because the chopsticks are too long, the food never reaches their mouths.

"In heaven, the image is exactly the same: Everyone is given an abundance of food, and their chopsticks are also a yard long. But in heaven, the people use their chopsticks to feed one another. A single act of compassion can instantly transform hell into heaven."[4]

We have plenty of opportunities to practice heart perspective. In a competitive world where so many people feel compelled to go straight for the jugular vein, we have the opportunity to go straight for the heart. You may be thinking, you may be speaking, you may be feeling, but see yourself doing all of this through your heart until you feel as though it is your heart (and not your head or your ego or your defense mechanisms) that is thinking, speaking and feeling. This takes practice, but it can be done.

Through heart perspective we consciously make an effort to relate to the beauty of the soul and not to the idiosyncrasies of the outer personality. We try not to judge another, for we never know what burden she is carrying—or whether we are correctly interpreting her actions. As Henry Wadsworth

Longfellow once wrote, "Every man has his secret sorrows which the world knows not; and oftentimes we call a man cold when he is only sad."

Sometimes we are so preoccupied with our tasks that we don't take time to approach life through the heart. Once forty professors from the United States visited Mother Teresa in Calcutta. One of them piped up, "Tell us something that will help us change our lives." He was probably not expecting the simple prescription she offered. "Smile at each other," she said. "Make time for each other, enjoy each other." In other words, remember the heart.

> *That mirror that shows reality is the heart.*
> —LAHIJI

Rumi gives some of the most eloquent and perceptive lessons on the heart that we will find anywhere. He shows us that heart perspective may be 180 degrees removed from the preconceptions of our mind. In one of Rumi's poems, Moses meets a shepherd who is spontaneously speaking to God. In his inspired monologue, the shepherd offers to fix God's shoes, wash his clothes and sweep his room for him. Moses is appalled and rebukes him, saying that such inappropriate familiarity sounds like he's chatting with his uncles.

The penitent shepherd wanders into the desert when suddenly God rebukes Moses for having separated the shepherd from him. God says that it's not the ways of worshiping that are important but whether there is a burning love within. "I don't hear the words," explains God. "I look inside."[5]

Through heart perspective we also see the challenges that come our way as "love ops"—moments when we are called to demonstrate love or to learn something new about loving. For Patrick,* life's challenges have become a series of wake-up calls to a higher love. At 37 he suffered the first of three heart attacks. Now 61, he has had three open-heart surgeries, nine bypasses and twenty cardiac catheterizations. When doctors recently performed a new experimental surgery on his heart, they weren't sure he would make it. But he did, even surviving a serious bout with pulmonary heart edema.

Patrick's doctors admit that he is alive by an incredible act of will. Patrick says that what has enabled him to survive is his quest for divine love. The physical challenges to his heart have sensitized him to the spiritual potential of his heart. Life, he has come to realize, is really only a prepa-

---

*The names in stories are changed except for public figures.

ration for eternity. "Everything that I've gone through physically," he says, "has helped me open up to my spirit. It's as if the deterioration of my physical heart has helped me discover the living structure of my spirit. And as my health deteriorates, my love grows."

Looking back to his earlier years, Patrick realizes that he was destroying himself emotionally. Like so many men of his generation, he says, in those days he was on a rocket ship to nowhere. "We were afraid of not accomplishing everything we thought our parents wanted us to accomplish," says Patrick. "Now I realize that a lot of those things I spent my energy on are not going with me. I'm not taking my car with me. I'm not taking my home with me. And as wonderful as my business is, I'm not taking that with me either. The only thing I will have is my spirit."

That awakening has given Patrick his new lease on life. It has also given him an intense desire to express more love whenever he can and a desire to pass on what he's learned. He especially wants to help his children develop a greater sense of their spirituality and understand how magical life can be when we focus on the heart. "They don't have to worry so much about competing," he says. "All they've got to do is be themselves and open up to the challenge of finding divine love in this lifetime."

HEART PERSPECTIVES

At the end of each section in this book under the heading "Heart Perspectives," we offer practical techniques you can use to increase your capacity to give and receive more love and to create your own alchemy of the heart.

• **Create your own heart ritual.** Maybe you do it before you get out of bed in the morning or just before you go to sleep. Start by simply concentrating on your heart. Take a few moments to close your eyes and feel the spiritual presence that dwells within your heart. This is your time to reconnect with your spiritual self and to remember your soul's inner vow made long ago to become a living transformer of love. Go back to this simple ritual throughout the day, especially when conditions tempt you to move away from the seat of love in your heart.

• **Practice centering in your heart.** As you go through the day, periodically bring your awareness to your heart. Try to consciously think, feel, act and even breathe as if you were doing all of these through your heart.

• **Find a simple prayer, affirmation or mantra** that helps you connect to your heart and to the heart of God, and make it a part of your spiritual practice each day. During the day if you feel the urge to criticize yourself or others, to get upset or to move out of your heart in some way, stop. Redirect your attention to your heart and recite your affirmation or prayer as many times as you wish. It can be as simple as one of those listed below.

O God, * *you are so magnificent!*

O Divine Presence,
    let me see as you would see,
    hear as you would hear
    and speak as you would speak.

Om Mani Padme Hum

(Pronounced Om Mah-nee Pud-may Hoom.) This ancient and popular Buddhist mantra for compassion means "Hail to the jewel in the lotus." The jewel in the lotus has been interpreted in many ways, including the unfolding of the jewel of spirituality or enlightenment within the lotus of awakened consciousness, the wedding of wisdom and compassion, and the awakening of the Buddha (or the Christ) within the heart.

---

*You can use whatever appellation for the Universal Spirit you are most comfortable with.

Stretch the Muscles of the Heart

Love is not effortless.
To the contrary, love is effortful.   —M. SCOTT PECK

"I don't have any real friends," Shelley admitted, explaining how lonely she had become over the years.

"Are you a friend to anyone?" I gently asked.

She hadn't expected that answer and stared back at me in silence while the truth sunk in: You can't have friends unless you are a friend yourself.

It's the same way with love. The secret to attracting what we want is to start to become it ourselves. Rather than desiring to be loved, *be* love. If you want to increase your capacity to give and receive more love, start by giving more love to others.

Stretch! Do something you don't want to do. That's what Saint Francis did—and it changed his life.

The son of a well-to-do merchant, Francis had always been terrified of lepers. He avoided them whenever he saw them coming and would even ask others to deliver his alms to them. One day, as Francis was riding his horse around a bend in the road, he came upon a leper covered with sores. The sight and stench of the wretched man repulsed him.

His first impulse was to turn his horse around and flee. He checked himself, suddenly realizing that he could not pretend to love God and yet turn his back on someone in need. This time, instead of letting his aversion get the upper hand, he opened his heart as well as his purse. Francis dismounted and as he reached out to give the leper alms, he kissed the man and embraced him.

Francis's encounter with the leper was a turning point in his life. He was transported by the experience and felt he had gained a victory over a great weakness. "Everything was so changed for me that what had seemed at first painful and impossible to overcome became easy and pleasant," he later wrote.

This is not just a tale from the life of a saint. It is a lesson in how to jump-start the alchemy of the heart. Is there a "leper" in your life who needs your love—someone who repulses you or something you just don't want to do? That person or situation is probably a messenger of love come to show you that your heart needs to stretch a little more in this or that direction.

As Rumi tells us, being human is like being "a

guest house." Every morning there is a new arrival, a new messenger. Greet even the sorrow that violently enters and carries away all your furniture, advises the poet, for this guest may be clearing space for something new and wonderful. "Be grateful for whoever comes," he says, "because each has been sent as a guide from beyond."[6]

Opening your heart to embrace the person or situation that pains you could be one of the most life-transforming experiences you'll ever have. It can also be one of the most courageous, for love takes courage and it takes will. Love takes courage because it forces us into unknown territory. Mark Prophet used to define courage as *coeur-age*—the coming of age of the heart (*coeur* in French). Courage is the development of the love and wisdom of the heart that emboldens us to take the action that is right, honorable and necessary, even if it is temporarily uncomfortable.

In *The Road Less Traveled,* M. Scott Peck aptly describes love as "the will to extend one's self for the purpose of nurturing one's own or another's spiritual growth." He says, "A genuinely loving individual will often take loving and constructive action toward a person he or she consciously dislikes, actually feeling no love toward the person at the time and perhaps even finding the person repugnant in some way."[7]

If we have stopped extending, if we have stopped giving because it is uncomfortable, then we have stopped loving. "I've found that I don't grow if I don't have to stretch," says Neil, who has a high-pressure job helping put on large conferences. When he's rushing to take care of the next crisis before it happens, there's often an attendee looking lost, needing help—needing love. Then comes the choice: to walk on by or to extend love.

"I've found that the tests of love come when I'm really tired," says Neil. "Someone needs help and it's inconvenient and it's the last thing I want to do. But doing it forces me out of my comfort zone. And if I can't get past the point of pain in doing it, the blessing never comes."

Like athletes training for the high jump, reaching a new level of heart mastery is at first a push. It takes practice. But as we keep stretching, we become more agile until we master that jump and we're ready to raise the bar again. In the realm of the heart, whenever we allow ourselves to move beyond the arbitrary limitations we have accepted, we expand our capacity to love.

Our soul wants us to exceed those limits and therefore we often unconsciously magnetize the people who will bring us face-to-face with the next bar. Relationships are notorious opportunities for stretching the muscles of the heart.

Like many newlyweds, Roberto didn't understand what was going on when the honeymoon suddenly came to a halt. Almost everything he did and said upset his wife, Maria. They couldn't figure out how to get over the next hurdle. After some heart-wrenching arguments and stony silences, they decided to embrace "the leper." It took a few long talks and some deep soul searching before the two of them began to understand the initiations of love they were facing.

> Look for a long time at what pleases you, and for a longer time at what pains you.
>
> —COLETTE

On the one hand, Maria realized that the roots of her discontent lay within and that she had some unrealistic expectations about how her new husband would fulfill her needs. She had to soften her heart and put herself in Roberto's shoes. A long-time bachelor, Roberto wasn't used to sharing his world with someone else, and he wasn't going to change overnight. For his part, Roberto realized that if he was to grow in love, he had to open his heart and become less self-centered.

"I never thought I would say it, but it's really a gift from God to be married to someone who won't let you stay the way you are," Roberto now says. "It's like we're both booting each other up the ladder into heaven."

Love certainly doesn't leave you where it finds you, and it won't let you leave others where you find them either. Take Clara and Lorraine Hale. One day on her way home from work, Lorraine had stopped to talk to her mother about her frustration working as a guidance counselor in the New York City public schools. "Lorraine, God put you on this earth for a reason," her mother had said. "He's going to reveal that reason to you. . . . Be still and listen with your heart so you'll know when He puts it before you."

On her way home, as she was waiting in heavy traffic for the light to change, Lorraine saw a disheveled young woman sitting on a wooden crate. The woman, who could barely keep her eyes open, was holding a tiny baby in her arms. The light changed and Lorraine continued on her way, but she couldn't get that baby out of her mind. A few blocks later she turned around, went back to that corner and parked her car. She handed the woman a note and said, "Here, go to this address. My mother will help."

The next morning, the woman and child arrived at Clara Hale's doorstep. Clara had raised dozens of children as a foster parent, but until then she had never taken in any right off the street. That stretch of the heart soon changed Clara's and Lorraine's lives dramatically. The same year, they founded Hale House in Harlem. It was the first nonprofit nursery in the country dedicated solely to the care of children of drug-addicted mothers.

The fragile children of Hale House come from prisons, hospitals, police precincts, welfare offices, clergy, social workers, relatives and sometimes the mothers themselves. The staff provides round-the-clock "love-care." Each child is given holistic nurturing, including nutrient-rich food prepared from scratch. In addition to caring for babies born addicted to drugs, Hale House cares for children infected with HIV or suffering from AIDS.

The Hales also founded Homeward Bound,

a program to help mothers recovering from drug addiction to enter back into society and take on their parental responsibilities. Clara passed on in 1992, and Lorraine continues their work.

"What we lacked in experiential know-how," says Lorraine, "we made up for with the greatest of all gifts one human can give another: love. It was sheer love, administered to these tiny victims of drug abuse, that brought miraculous results. I'm talking about the kind of love that outlasts weeks of torture a baby goes through while ridding its body of drugs received in the womb."[8]

You don't have to go far to find someone who needs your love. In fact, most of the time there is someone right outside your own doorstep (or inside your home) who is crying out to you to open your heart a little more.

HEART PERSPECTIVES

• **Identify the next stretch** that will help you open your heart a little more. Who or what are the messengers in your life that are asking you to stretch? What are they trying to tell you? What must you do to make that next stretch?

- **Embrace the "leper."** Is there someone who annoys you or something that you don't want to do because it will force you out of your comfort zone? How can you open your heart to embrace this "leper" in your life?

 ## "I Love, Therefore…"

If a friend is in trouble, don't annoy him
by asking if there is anything you can do.
Think up something appropriate and do it.
—*EDGAR WATSON HOWE*

The language of the heart may be poetic, but the actions of the heart are extremely practical. When we love, what we must do and what we must let go of become obvious. You say to yourself, "I love, therefore I can't carry around this anger or pride or selfishness or jealousy. I am love, therefore I can't hold on to this resentment or bitterness that saps my creative energy. I am love, therefore I can't have this condition in my life stopping me from doing what I must do."

What are you willing to do and how are you

willing to change in order to be love in action? It's a powerful exercise to write down *"I am love, therefore_____"* and then fill in the blank. First, list the things in your life that have to go so you can love more, whether it's pessimism, fear, selfishness, feeling sorry for yourself or a lack of self-confidence. Maybe you need to give up staying late at work so you can spend more time with your family.

I am love, therefore this self-concern has to go! This worry has to go! This false sense of inadequacy has to go! I am a pillar of love, therefore I invite the angels into my life to help me clear this condition of consciousness that stands in the way of the full flowering of my heart!

Next write down the positive vision of what things will look like once you have loved. When you are love, what is your universe like? What is your life like? What is your heart like? How do you treat yourself? How do you treat others?

Then affirm aloud with all of your being the love commitments you have written down: *I am love, therefore...*

The "therefore" will be different for each of us. For correspondent Kurt Schork and cameraman

Miguel Gil Moreno, the "therefore" was to travel where few would venture—to war zones around the world like Bosnia, Kosovo and Chechnya. They risked their lives on the front lines to sensitize the international community to what was really happening at these hot spots. In May 2000, they were killed in Sierra Leone in what was probably a rebel ambush, victims of the bloody civil war they were covering.

> *Giving is the highest expression of potency.*
>
> —ERICH FROMM

Both men were profoundly aware of the risks as well as the importance of their jobs. "Miguel was doing the job he loved and died doing the work he felt ordained for," said Miguel's mother. "He felt his mission was to give voice to those who did not have one."[9]

For Lesia Cartelli, the "therefore" was to face her greatest fear and turn it into her greatest strength. When she was nine, a furnace exploded while she was playing hide-and-seek in her grandparents' basement. Lesia suffered second- and third-degree burns on 50 percent of her body. Although she survived, her face was puckered with scar tissue and she was afraid of fires and natural gas. As an adult, she hated gassing up her car or even watching a fire scene in a movie.

Lesia counseled children who were burn victims and spoke at fairs and schools, but she never faced her fear head-on—that is, until she decided to take part in a training exercise for fire fighting with the help of her future husband, fire captain Bruce Cartelli. After four tries with Bruce by her side, she was finally able to crawl to a set of burning stairs, open the nozzle of the fire hose and spray the flames until they died. She couldn't stop crying for eight days afterward, as she released the pent-up emotions of twenty-six years.

Today Lesia says that so much good has come from her "facing the dragon." Her passion is to assist children and adults who have burn injuries and other traumas to heal "inside and out." She speaks at conferences, consults with burn camps internationally, and draws from her personal experiences to design support systems within camps for burn-injured children. And she is no longer afraid to light a log fire or a barbecue.

"Whatever your fears are, embrace them," she advises. "When you face fear head-on, it dissolves."[10] She also tells others that everything in life carries a potential blessing and that her scars have given her an incredible sense of purpose and have shaped her life's work.

For Aaron Feuerstein, owner of Malden Mills, a textile mill near Boston, the "therefore" was sacrificing short-term gain to help those who needed him most. In December 1995, on the night of his seventieth birthday, three of his factories at the mill burned to the ground. A boiler explosion had set off a fire that left only sections of brick walls and smoking piles of twisted metal. Malden Mills was the biggest employer in Methuen, Massachusetts, and some three thousand jobs were threatened. What's worse, it was just two weeks before Christmas.

On the night of the fire, Aaron made three promises to his employees. He promised them each a $275 Christmas bonus. He promised that he would continue to pay his workers' wages for the month and keep up their health insurance for three months. And he promised that he would rebuild the plant.

His employees were shocked. They knew that Aaron could have thrown up his hands, taken the $300 million in insurance money and run. If he had, his three thousand employees and their families, not to mention all the businesses that supported them in that town, would have been in trouble. Instead, with incredible faith and determination, Aaron put his own future on the line for them.

"What kind of an ethic is it that a CEO is prepared to hurt 3,000 people who are his employees [and] an entire city of many more thousands... in order for him to have a short-term gain," said Aaron. "It's unthinkable."[11] Aaron's employees worked at top speed to get the mill up and running. Only three months later, production in one of the plants that hadn't been destroyed actually doubled.

Aaron knew instinctively that when we open our heart, when we affirm that nothing will stand in the way of our expression of love, both inner and outer forces will rally in answer to our call. As long as the motive of our heart is pure and what we ask for is in accordance with the divine plan, God will send invisible helpers to assist us in our job of love.

Aaron also knew another secret to heart mastery: when we give, we adjust our gifts (the gifts of our talents, our actions and our resources) not to what we think we can afford but to the size of the need. It's like the old story about the rabbi who used to entertain many poor people in his home. At a time when food was expensive, the rabbi noticed that the loaves on his guests' plates were smaller than usual. He went straight to the cooks and told them to make the loaves larger to adjust to hunger rather than to price.

Most of the time our acts of love do not gain public notice. Nevertheless, it is the small things we do, one by one by one, that add up to a dramatic difference in someone's life. As Mother Teresa said, "We do no great things; we only do small things with great love." "Good people follow virtue," taught Confucius, "building on the small to attain the great."

> It has long been an axiom of mine that little things are infinitely the most important.
> —SIR ARTHUR CONAN DOYLE

Of course, giving to others doesn't mean we should suppress our own needs. Love is sacrifice, but it's not destroying yourself in the process. You can't divide yourself in a thousand pieces and still have something of substance left over to give to others.

Sometimes it's hard to give yourself permission to set boundaries or to do something for yourself first, especially when others are tugging on you. But if you are to provide meaningful support to others, you have to give yourself permission to do those things that will bank the fires of your heart so you can use that fire to warm and nurture others.*

HEART PERSPECTIVES

• **What are your "therefores"?** Take some time to meditate on and then write down what you are willing to leave behind and what you are willing to do in order to be love in action (as outlined on page 25). Then affirm aloud your commitments to love: *I am love, therefore _____.* Put your affirmations where you will see them every day, and say them aloud at least once a day.

Schedule time in your daily planner to make good on your love commitments. As Stephen Covey says, "The key is not to prioritize what's on your schedule, but to schedule your priorities."

• **Adjust your gifts to the size of the need.** Are there areas in your life where you need to readjust

---

*See also "Nurturing Yourself," pages 46–54.

what you give—from both your spiritual and material resources—to the size of the need rather than to what you think you can afford?

• **Confront your fears.** Is there something you are afraid to face that is keeping you from making progress? Ask yourself how you could move through that fear and what support you would need.

PART TWO

EMPOWERING
the Heart

*Love is a creative force and power.
Once you realize that you are a co-creator
with God, your life changes. You begin to realize,
"This is an awesome responsibility. What am I going
to do with my power to create? I've got three-score
and ten and maybe a little more to do it in.
What will I create?"*

Connecting with Compassion

My friends have made the story of my life…
turned my limitations into beautiful privileges.
—HELEN KELLER

Dorothy Canfield Fisher once said, "A mother is not a person to lean on but a person to make leaning unnecessary." That's because a real mother is compassionate, and compassion empowers. Compassion supports but it doesn't smother. It comforts but it doesn't cushion.

Although the words *compassion* and *sympathy* are sometimes used interchangeably, making a distinction can help us better understand compassionate love and its counterfeit. Compassion is empowering because it helps us learn the spiritual lessons inherent in all our challenges. Compassion doesn't blame others for the circumstances we find ourselves in but shows us that it's our reaction to those circumstances that matters most. Compassion invites us to climb to a higher vantage point so we can meet our challenges from a new level.

Human sympathy, on the other hand, allows us to play the role of victim. It encourages us to indulge in self-pity and to remain right where we are. Sympathy tempts us to escape from reality rather than face it.

Sympathy may feel good for the moment, but in the long run it doesn't help us grow spiritually. If a parent sympathetically spoils his child and cushions him from the challenges and hard work it takes to mature and blossom, that child may never grow up. No matter how old we are, if we don't engage with our heart lessons, our heart will never mature.

Like many parents, Susan learned firsthand that the best way to treat her son was with compassion and not sympathy. In the process, she received some very important heart lessons of her own. For years her son, Michael, struggled to cope emotionally. At times he was able to work at a job, but at 21 he reached a point where he depended on her for everything. He couldn't even perform simple chores and wanted to stay home all the time.

After talking with both friends and professionals, Susan finally saw that Michael needed psychological help. She also came to realize that she and

Michael had to make a serious decision—should he continue to live at home or move into a group home where he would have professional care?

"I was working out of my home and I could have taken care of him, and that is what he wanted," says Susan. "But it wasn't what was best for him, because I had become his crutch. I was hindering his growth. That was a big one. You think you're giving your children the best option because you're making it comfortable for them. But it doesn't work like that."

Michael reluctantly moved into a group home some 70 miles away and Susan visits him every week. After just three months, he has improved tremendously. "I realized that putting some space between us was actually the best thing I could do for him," admits Susan. "It was a higher love."

It was also the best thing Susan could do for herself. She's now able to take time to nurture herself and work on her own spiritual growth, and she has found new ways of serving others. She has even decided to make a career change. "I was holding myself back as well as my son," she acknowledges. "The most painful choices are sometimes the ones that help us grow the most."

It's not always easy to tell when we are caught in a cycle of sympathy rather than compassion, especially in close relationships. How do we know for sure? For one thing, compassion energizes and sympathy tends to de-energize. Compassion feels supportive and strengthening while sympathy feels stifling.

In a relationship based on compassion, both people have room to be who they really are. They respect each other's needs and help each other blossom. Compassion, because it is love, fosters growth. In a relationship based on sympathy, however, one or both people feel frustrated, hedged in, noncreative. They begin to lose a sense of their own identity. Sympathetic relationships breed codependence.

> *If you want others to be happy, practice compassion. If you want to be happy, practice compassion.*
>
> —THE DALAI LAMA

Erika Chopich and Margaret Paul describe a codependent as one who "gives power to others to define himself or herself." They say that codependents "experience their sense of self and worth *through* others. They allow others to define them, and make others responsible for their feelings."[1]

Melody Beattie says that a codependent is a person "who has let another person's behavior affect him or her, or who is obsessed with controlling that person's behavior."[2]

It's normal to care about others, but it's not healthy when our concerns about others become self-destructive. As Beattie says, codependents tend to worry themselves sick over others or try to help in ways that don't really help. They desperately try to avoid hurting other people's feelings and end up hurting themselves. They say yes when they really mean no.[3] "So many people, under the illusion of being nice," writes John Gray, "sacrifice too much of who they are and thus lose their ability to truly love and get the love they need."[4]

There are a number of good books as well as health-care professionals who can help us get to the root of these self-destructive patterns and create healthy relationships. From a spiritual perspective, one of the most important keys to a good relationship is to cultivate our unique relationship with our Higher Self and with God, and to help our partner do the same. "To love another person," said Søren Kierkegaard, "is to help them love God." That strong, inner spiritual connection is what will ultimately sustain us on our journey of love.

If we allow someone to depend solely on us to bring them happiness, stability and self-worth, we aren't doing them any favors. We can and should encourage, support and strengthen others, but nothing we do can replace another's own upward reach. On the path of self-mastery, each person has to build his or her own personal relationship with God.

HEART PERSPECTIVES

• **Apply the lessons of compassion.** In your interactions with others, what have you learned about the empowerment of compassion versus the stifling and de-energizing nature of sympathy? How can you apply these lessons in your current relationships and interactions?

• **Assess the quality of your relationships.** Make a list of the key relationships in your life now. Is there anyone you are overly concerned about or anyone who is overly protective of you? Is there anyone you need to support in a more compassionate, empowering way rather than a sympathetic, dependent way?

Build a Momentum

There is only work and love in life....
If we are fortunate, we love our work.
If we are wise, we are willing to work at love.

—NOAH BEN SHEA

There will never be a list of do's and don'ts for how to make yourself love more—no ready-made formulas. We each have to discover for ourselves what is the key that unleashes the wellspring of love within us.

Yet one thing the masters of love do tell us is that it becomes easier to love when we make it a habit. They say the love that flows with spontaneity is the love that has been generated through habit. Loving is a momentum, and you gain momentum by doing something every day and doing it when it's not easy. By priming the pump of the fount of love, your heart will be ready on a moment's notice to soothe a troubled heart, a tired body or a soul in pain.

When people need love, they need it now. When they are in distress or despair, when they are sick or suicidal, they need an immediate transfer from your heart to their heart. If your baby is crying, you don't wait until you're finished what you're doing to find out what's wrong. The same principle applies whenever you are dedicated to increasing the flow of love through your heart. You're on God's hot line, and he can call you anytime of the day or night and say, "I've got somebody in need. Go and help that person."

> *We are what we repeatedly do. Excellence, then, is not an act, but a habit.*
>
> —ARISTOTLE

When we love, we don't say, "I care about you, but it's just too inconvenient to do this or that right now." Love is measured by the actions we take, and it means the most when we are able to give it consistently under extraordinary circumstances.

U Tin U, one of the leaders of the democracy movement in Burma, understood this principle. In circumstances that would have caused most people to lash out or become bitter, he resolved to keep his love alive. He had been in prison for three years and had almost served his full term when he was retried and sentenced again—for seven years. He was finally released in 1995.

Speaking of his imprisonment and solitary

confinement, he said that even though he was severely restricted, he found ways to keep his spirit alive. "My hut within the prison compound was completely encircled with barbed wire. I was indoors all the time," he said. "And the wire was a constant reminder of how precious freedom was. . . . The loss of one's freedom can inspire reflection on the preciousness of freedom. This filled me with joy. . . .

"I would also regularly recite the Buddha's discourses in Pali as well as study them, which inspired me greatly. In addition, a small book containing quotations of Jesus was smuggled through to me. I very much liked his attitude of forgiveness and sincerity."

During his imprisonment, U Tin U's wife would visit and bring him food. How precious her visits and her gifts must have been. Yet U Tin U went out of his way to share this food with his jailors and even some of the military intelligence personnel. "I wanted to overcome any feelings of seeing them as the 'enemy' so I tried to make a practice of sharing a little of my food with them," he said. "They too had a hard life in prison."[5]

U Tin U instinctively knew that if we build a momentum of love, our heart will never shut down. If we continually allow a flood tide of love to flow out from our heart to others, the gates of our heart will never close.

If we could see a picture of a magnanimous heart at spiritual levels, it would look convex— expansive, brimming with light, constantly emanating light. When we are not emitting the strong, pure love of the heart, when we are so self-absorbed that we cannot give, the heart will become concave—caved in, sunken, depressed.

> *It is only possible to live happily ever after on a day-to-day basis.*
> —MARGARET BONNANO

The masters of love also tell us that if we can keep our heart open, even when it is painful, we can be an agent of compassion and positive change on earth. The ancient Jewish mystical tradition Kabbalah teaches that every one of us individually contributes to the condition of the world. Moment by moment, we either increase the force of good on the planet or we increase the weight of negativity.

Kabbalah also teaches that evil in and of itself has no power. It is literally our negative thoughts, feelings, words and deeds that empower evil.

Conversely, the good that we do deprives evil of its power and compels the divine world to send blessings to our world.[6] And when enough of us embody the quality of love, one by one by one, the world will become a loving place. As Gandhi once said, "It is my firm faith that we can conquer the whole world by truth and love."

HEART PERSPECTIVES

• **Prime the pump.** Are there challenging circumstances in your life that you can use as opportunities to keep love alive? What exactly can you do to keep up a momentum of love in these situations?

• **Give a transfer of love.** Reflect on your interactions with others today. Was there someone who needed a transfer of love from your heart? Did you take the time to meet that need? If not, how can you now provide the love and support he needs?

♥ Nurturing Yourself

Giving ourselves what we need means we become...
our personal counselor, confidante, spiritual advisor,
partner, best friend, and caretaker.... If we listen to
ourselves and our Higher Power, we will not be misled.

—*MELODY BEATTIE*

Carey was at a crossroads. She was desperately trying to figure out why she could never stay focused on a direction for her life. During a long bus trip back to her hometown, she had time to think—a lot of time. In the silent recesses of her heart, she called out to God and to the inner wisdom of her own Higher Self to help her understand.

By the time she stepped off the bus, Carey had a startling revelation. For the first time in her life, she saw that the reason she hadn't been able to focus and to achieve her goals was that she had a deep belief that she *couldn't* achieve them. She had never allowed herself to get on track because she was afraid she would fail.

Sometimes, like Carey, our lack of self-confidence or lack of consistency has deeper roots. It may go back to a crisis in love—a crisis in self-love.

Do we love and appreciate ourselves? If we don't love ourselves, we will sabotage our own spiritual, emotional and professional progress. We won't allow ourselves to go higher simply because we don't believe we are capable *or worthy* of going higher.

This spiritual malady (often reinforced by misguided parents, peers, authority figures and even the media) will infect us with the false belief that we don't deserve that fulfilling job, that meaningful relationship, that beautiful home or even those exalting spiritual experiences that we need and deserve. In addition, if we don't love ourselves, we will short-circuit our ability to give love and to receive love. In fact, we may fail, whether consciously or unconsciously, just to prove that we are unworthy.

"Not only does this unconscious self-hatred get in the way of expressing love, it also interferes with receiving love," writes Dr. Harville Hendrix. "You cannot feel worthy of accepting love if you unconsciously hate yourself or even hate some parts of yourself."[7]

Those who are spiritually inclined tend to hold high standards for themselves and to be overly critical of themselves. They also tend to be extremely sensitive to what others say. While we should be realistic about the areas in our life where we need to improve, we also have to be realistic about the nature of life and spirituality. Life is a path, and spirituality is a process. Today we are not who we were yesterday, just as we are not now who we will be tomorrow.

When we deal with children, we know that they are engaged in a continual process of growth and refinement, and we don't criticize them if they make a mistake. Yet we don't always translate that process into our adult life and treat our soul in the same way.

The soul is our inner child, still in the process of refinement, still unfolding her full potential. No matter what our inner child is experiencing now, we can love our soul as she walks the path of becoming whole. For what's most important is not how far we still have to go but *whether we are fully engaged in the process.* Can we listen to what our heart tells us is the next step on our path and take it?

Maybe we're a little like Lisa, and we don't want to face what our heart has to tell us. Lisa was a single mom. When she wasn't taking care of her children, she was working—day and night. She kept herself so busy that she never had time to self-reflect. What she later realized was that for years she had been harboring a lot of guilt, and she was doing everything she could to avoid facing it.

"It's hard to take a good look at yourself," she admits. "It's easier to say, give me something I can throw myself into—a good project that will take me a year to complete. Give me something that will require all of my energy so I don't have to think about my problems. But what's really happening is you're cutting yourself off from your emotions."

After her children had grown up and left home, Lisa had some time on her hands. What do I do now? she thought. The silence served as a wake-up call. It helped her see that she had never taken the time to get to know her core self. "You can be so busy with your career and your children that you don't take time to figure out who you really are and who you want to become," she says. "You don't take the time to ask yourself what *you* really need."

Lisa's newfound solitude became a time for self-reflection. It helped her discover one of the reasons she had avoided the silence for so long. She saw that for years she had been keeping her parents at a distance because she blamed them for disciplining her. At the same time, she felt guilty for being hard to handle as a child. Now she has started communicating with her parents more frequently and has come to appreciate how beautiful and loving they are. "I've reconnected at a real heart level with my parents and it's opened up a whole new world in my heart," she says.

Lisa has also worked at changing her rhythms, purposely slowing down. "I had to give myself permission to nourish my soul," she says. "Now I take time to stop and look at the sunset and appreciate little things. There is a pansy grow-ing in the middle of my yard and I get so much out of it every time I pass it. Normally I would be run-ning to my car and I wouldn't even notice."

> *Take time to come home to yourself every day.*
> —ROBIN CASARJIAN

If you want to empower your heart, start by listening to what your heart says you need at that moment. It could be anything from stopping to smell the flowers to getting a back rub to ex-ploring a career change. Listening to our heart is empowering because it's the first step to taking responsibility for our own needs.

"If you want to love, take the time to listen to your heart," advises author and Buddhist meditation teacher Jack Kornfield. "In most ancient and wise cultures, it is a regular practice for people to talk to their heart.... In the heart of each of us, there is a voice of knowing, a song that can remind us of what we most value and long for, what we have known since we were a child."[8]

Sometimes we deny the voice of our heart. We think that taking care of our own needs is selfish. But when we take care of our own needs, we are recharging our spiritual and physical reserves so that we in turn can give more to others. If we don't nurture ourselves, we can't really value and nurture others. Jesus said, "Love thy neighbor *as* thyself"—in other words, love your neighbor *as you would love* yourself. If we can't love ourselves, how can we then love others?

Before Gautama Buddha could begin his life's mission, he had to learn a serious lesson about self-nurturing. For six years he practiced intense self-denial and bodily mortifications, becoming so weak that he finally fainted. After he recovered, he realized that by denying his bodily needs he was undermining what he most wanted to accomplish. "With a weakened body," he later explained, "I could not devote my last existence to compassion."

He needed to care for himself before he could care for others.

We too must take care of ourselves so we can deliver compassion to others. When you need time alone to gather your inner forces, take it. When you need time out to refocus on what is priority in your life, take it. And when you need nurturing, don't hand the job over to someone else.

> *Love is, above all,*
> *the gift of oneself.*
> —JEAN ANOUILH

If we look to someone else for love to make up for the fact that we don't love and honor ourselves, we can fall into the dangerous trap of idolatry. We can say to ourselves (sometimes over and over again), "Ah, here's the most wonderful person I've ever met in the whole world. At last I've found the person who will love me perfectly. Now all my problems will be solved." This is a trap and a formula for disaster.

When you love yourself, you take responsibility for your life's direction and for fulfilling your personal needs. Jan, for example, was living in Florida close to Disney World—near "Mickey Mouse," as she says. She had a good job but she loathed the coldness of the cities and the commute on crowded highways. "People just didn't smile enough and everybody was too busy to pay attention to anybody else," she says.

Once a year Jan made the great escape to her favorite valley in Montana for vacation. That had been her vacation spot for ten years. She was so enchanted with it that she had even bought a second home there.

Finally the hustle and bustle of the city became too much. Jan stopped and asked herself what may prove to be the most important question of her life: "If I only had six months to live, where would I go and what would I do?" It didn't take long for her heart to answer that question. "Since you never know how long you have," she says, "I decided I had better make that move now."

While her plans were in motion, she met and fell in love with the man of her dreams. But she was still convinced that she had to move. Within a few months Jan was living in Montana, her fiancé was making plans to join her, and she had landed a great job. Although it paid less than her old job, money was not her primary concern. "It's a quality of life issue for me," she says. "And after all, fly-fishing costs less than going to see Mickey

Mouse, and it's a lot more fun."

What's crucial about this story is not that Jan moved out of the city, because for some of us the city is what we need. What's crucial is that she asked the right questions and listened to her heart's answer—and that she is taking responsibility for nurturing herself.

HEART PERSPECTIVES

• **Make a list of what you love about yourself.** If you have a hard time doing this, ask others what they appreciate about you.

• **Check in with your heart.** Ask your heart what you need *right now* to be more balanced and at peace.

• **Face the tough questions.** If you only had six months to live, what would you focus your time on? What would your goals be? How would you live your life?

• **Are there any boundaries that you need to draw** in order to nurture yourself so you can better nurture others? How can you lovingly communicate those boundaries to others?

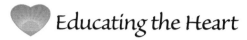# Educating the Heart

There is no reality except the one contained within us. That is why so many people live such an unreal life. They take the images outside them for reality and never allow the world within to assert itself. —HERMANN HESSE

The host of a radio show in Chicago was talking with me about what it takes to attain union with God. "Just look how serious and disciplined the rabbis are," he was saying. "From the time they are young boys, they study many hours a day. They submerge themselves in the ancient texts, the scriptures and the Talmud. They become experts in the law and the scriptures."

This, of course, is a discipline that takes place in many religions, but it seemed to me that the host was implying that the studious ones, by virtue of their erudition and mental discipline, would become superior beings—and that this is what it takes to attain union with God.

"Yet you could have all of that knowledge and no love," I replied. "Knowledge in and of itself does not guarantee our entrée into the kingdom of heaven or our spiritual attainment or our union with God. What does is how much we love."

Discussions like this have probably been going on for aeons. In fact, in Mark Twain's delightful *Diary of Adam and Eve,* Eve laments in her musings about Adam, "I wish I could make him understand that a loving good heart is riches, and riches enough, and that without it intellect is poverty." Wisdom is a wonderful virtue. But unless our wisdom is fused with love and with the divine will, our intellect is spiritually impotent.

That lesson is one our society will be forced to master in this new millennium. Technology and science are accelerating at record speeds. What about the development of our hearts? Can we balance our scientific advances with a commensurate development of the heart that will enable us to make wise choices about issues like genetic engineering, our environment, or whether we use communications technology to inform and liberate or to control and regulate. Will we be able to employ enough love and wisdom to restrain the temptation to abuse power?

How we as a society meet these challenges depends on how we as individuals develop our heart. Confucius taught that developing the heart was key to setting the world in order. He said that to put the world in order, we must first put the nation in order. To put the nation in order, we must first put the family in order. To put the family in order, we must first cultivate our personal life.

And to cultivate our personal life, he said, we must become attuned to our heart.

> *Although intelligence is useful, it needs to be returned to the spirit. This is called the great harmony.*
>
> —HUAI-NAN-TZU

Do we teach our children to attune to their heart? Whether our children are able to freely express the finest qualities of the heart is a harbinger of the future. For many years I have been seriously concerned about the quality of our educational systems. I have been concerned that our children have ample opportunity to balance the development of their mind and the skills of their hands with what I have called the education of the heart.

Educating the heart allows us to fulfill our full spiritual potential. Educating the heart shows us how to rely on our own inner faculties and our own inner resources to meet the challenges at hand. Educating the heart increases the capacity of the soul to journey beyond herself—to probe the outer reaches of the universe as well as the inner-most depths of being.

If we are taught only to emphasize empirical ways of approaching a situation, then our analyt-ical brain becomes the sole instrument we depend on to shape our lives. Yet we have been endowed with so much more. Our heart and soul are con-tinually sensing, intuiting and perceiving what can-not be explained by empirical evidence. Things that don't make sense to the intellect make perfect sense to the heart and soul. If we don't pay atten-tion to and fine-tune the delicate instruments of our inner life, our innate spiritual abilities will re-main dormant.

Mark Prophet and I were so concerned about the missing elements in our public education sys-tem that in 1970 we founded Montessori Inter-national so that our children and many others who came to our school could receive a truly holistic education. At one time, our school had programs for preschoolers through high school.

Every precious little one must be given the maximum opportunity to understand the science of being. Each one must be taught how to listen with the heart and move with those inner promptings of the soul that will guide them on the course of their immortal destiny. This requires teachers to mentor rather than monitor. It requires teachers to step back and facilitate but not control the unfolding of the mind or the heart intelligence that is unique to each student.

In actuality, the only true educators are God and the indwelling spirit. All other teachers are substitutes, there to assist us until we learn to listen to the wisdom of our own heart and soul and higher mind.

> *You cannot teach a man anything; you can only help him find it within himself.*
> —GALILEO

Educating the heart prepares us to become living transformers of love. We learn to intuitively sense what others need, and we learn to meet that need with exactly what is required at that moment. That alchemical formula always comes from the heart.

HEART PERSPECTIVES

• Educate the heart every chance you can get. At one time or another, in one position or another, we all have the opportunity to teach someone something.

Think about a situation in your life right now where you are a teacher. How can you better use that opportunity to guide and mentor rather than to control? How can you creatively find new ways to educate the heart as well as the mind?

• **Appreciate the wisdom of your heart.** When faced with a problem that has no logical solution, take time to go into your heart and ask your Higher Self to activate the divine intelligence of your heart and reveal the answer you are seeking. Then listen for your heart's answer. Be patient, for it may come immediately or it may unfold in the hours or days ahead.

 **Heart Power**

Of all strong things nothing is so strong,
so irresistible, as divine love.   —WILLIAM LAW

Mahatma Gandhi was not a big man, but there's no question that he was a powerful one, powerful enough to lead a nation to independence. Gandhi's power didn't come from size, position or title. It came from love. He once wrote, "I hold myself to be incapable of hating any being on earth. By a long course of prayerful discipline, I have ceased for over forty years to hate anybody. I know this is a big claim. Nevertheless, I make it in all humility."

Heart power far outweighs any other kind of power. That is why the sages of East and West say that it doesn't take a lot of people to create spiritual transformation. It takes only a few very powerful hearts to ignite a conflagration. "The world," said André Gide, "will be saved by one or two people" —by you and me, right where we are.

When we love, purely for the sake of loving and not with any ulterior motive, God entrusts us with more power because he trusts us to use that power wisely. Larry, for instance, is amazed at how successful his health-food store in New York City has become. "I don't really know why. I'm not a businessman or an accountant," he says. His store is doing so well that people wonder why he doesn't expand or start a second one. But Larry hasn't gone that route because to him making more money isn't the measure of success. Heart contact is.

"My business is wonderful because it gives me the opportunity to work with people who are genuinely trying to help themselves," says Larry. "It's what separates this business from the local grocery store or any other retail operation—that unique moment when you have an opportunity to help people who in some cases are desperately looking for an answer to a serious illness. I find so much joy working with these people. I couldn't even think of taking advantage of them. My only concern is how we can continue to serve the people who come to us for help."

Larry's genuine concern and heart power are infectious. One evening as the young girl who works at his store was leaving work, she exuberantly told her co-workers how much she loved working at that store and working with each of them. It's not something you often hear in the workplace, and it made an impact on Larry. "There is no bottom line or peer esteem that could possibly come close to equaling love shared from the heart," he says. The love he shares from his heart is what naturally brings more love and abundance to his doorstep. It gives him heart power.

Pure love always brings power; for the more we love, the more powerfully our heart can affect other hearts. Paradoxically, as we receive more power, it is always a test of how much more we can love. The tests come in many guises. How do we treat the children in our family? How do we treat those who depend on us at home or at work? How do we use money and what do we spend it on? How do we use the authority we have been given —to serve others or to serve our ego?

Have you ever watched a seemingly gentle person, or even yourself, suddenly become transformed when given a certain amount of authority or responsibility? Before that new title or position, he looked like a saint. After-

> *The man of true greatness never loses his child's heart.*
> —MENCIUS

wards, a startling metamorphosis took place. Without an infusion of love, power can quickly become out of balance. And each new increment of power demands a greater infusion of love.

In other words, the only people who can successfully handle power are those who truly love. When you love, you develop an enormous sensitivity to life. You understand people, you understand their suffering, you understand their needs. When you love, you have the capacity to put yourself inside another's heart, and it hurts you to see another part of life get hurt. Therefore you use your power for compassion rather than control.

When we are in the midst of a test of love and we're slipping out of balance, there will always be something or someone who holds up a mirror to show us that our halo has become a bit crooked. In one of his poems, Rumi relates a parable about Solomon. He tells us that the king, who had the responsibility of judging his people, was disrupting the community by his thoughts. Eight times in a row Solomon's crown slid off the top of his head.

At last, the king talked to his crown and asked why it kept sliding down over his eyes. "When your power loses compassion," replied the crown, "I have to show what such a condition looks like." The wise king knelt and asked for forgiveness and at once the crown centered itself on his head.

At the conclusion of the poem, Rumi says that even the wisdom of one like Solomon or Plato "can wobble and go blind." He advises us: "*Listen* when your crown reminds you of what makes you cold toward others, as you pamper the greedy energy inside."[9] The test is not whether or not we can always stop the crown from slipping, because it will slip from time to time as we learn our lessons of love. The real test is: Can we acknowledge that it has slipped—and do we have enough love and humility to do what it takes to set it straight again?

HEART PERSPECTIVES

• **Learn from the tests of love.** Think of an example in your life when you were given an increment of power (as a parent, supervisor, project leader, et cetera). What was the corresponding test of love? What did you learn from that experience?

• **Look for the mirror.** Is there something or someone in your life who is a mirror, trying to show you where your use of power is out of balance with your loving compassion? How can you come back to center?

♥ Cultivate Gratitude

But listen to me: for one moment, quit being sad.
Hear blessings dropping their blossoms
around you. God.   —*RUMI*

Sharon was hiking with a friend high in the mountains when suddenly she was having trouble breathing. She was also running out of water and it was a long way down the mountain. "I didn't know how I was going to do it," she says.

Then Sharon heard a voice within her: *"Start saying to yourself everything you can think of that you are thankful for."* She began doing this and she kept doing it all the way down the mountain. "As I named one thing after another, I felt stronger and stronger, and I was able to make it down to the point where I could start to breathe normally again." Whenever Sharon is in a tough situation, she goes back to that key—she focuses on what she is grateful for, and that's what gets her through the eye of the needle.

Gratitude is strengthening because when we are grateful we establish a figure-eight flow of love from our heart to the heart of God. And when we send love and gratitude to God, light and blessings return to us. If we don't take a moment in our busy day to feel and express our profound gratitude to the spiritual Source that continuously gives us breath and life and opportunity, we are not tapping the tremendous resource of energy that is available to us at any hour of the day or night.

Sometimes we fail to make the most of the blessings we have been given because we dwell on the negatives instead of noticing the richness of our life. Something beautiful happens and all we can think of is the one thing that went wrong. Gratitude can help us gain back our heart perspective— the perspective that whatever is happening in our life, it is an opportunity, even a gift, that can help us open our heart and grow.

When we consciously cultivate gratitude, we get into the habit of seeing the positives. We don't take things apart before they've even had a chance to breathe the breath of life. We are naturally more balanced and at peace, and therefore we criticize less and we blame less. We make the most of what we have, and we enjoy life more.

Andrea Bocelli has learned to practice the art of gratitude and heart perspective. The phenomenal appeal of this popular singer has as much to do with the warmth of his heart as with the quality of his voice. In addition to his recording career and concert appearances, Andrea has a full life. He lives with his wife and two children in Tuscany, where he grew up. He skis and rides bicycles. He loves horseback riding and has trained horses.

> *[Love] is to learn from everything, to see the gifts of God and the generosity of God in everything.*
>
> —SHEIKH MUZAFFER

What makes all this so poignant is that Andrea has been blind since age 12. His inner strength is a reflection of his parents' fortitude. They forced him to face reality— the reality of his blindness as well as the reality of his vast potential. If anyone dared call him "poor little boy," his mother reacted like lightning. When the young Andrea asked if he would be able to see a certain house when he was older, she told him no, "but you will be able to see other things that we are not able to see."

As a child, he went on a pilgrimage to Lourdes and prayed to the Blessed Mother inside the grotto. On the way out of the grotto he confided to a friend of the family, a priest who had accompanied them, that he had not prayed to be healed of his blindness. Instead, he had asked for serenity. Now, his mother says, Andrea gives that serenity to many people who suffer, because his voice "consoles and brings light." She says, "I thank our Lord that Andrea lives in the same manner in which he sings, with an open heart."[10]

Andrea admits that he has a fascination for things that are difficult. Before his singing career took off, Andrea studied law and worked as a defense lawyer for a year. Finally his real passion pulled him in another direction. "Singing was my destiny," he says. He performed in piano bars by night and studied music by day. In 1992, he began his leap into the limelight when a demo tape he made reached the ears of Pavarotti, who was taken with the young tenor.

His new challenge is the opera, where he has had to learn to navigate around the stage as he both acts and sings. In a recent interview with Barbara Walters, Andrea said he doesn't think about the things he can't do but focuses on what he can do. He does not feel sorry for himself. There are many people who look at everything but don't really see anything, he explained. And there are other people who cannot look at anything but can see everything. "I don't look," he said, "but I see."

When we have gratitude, we see with our heart. This is the secret that the little prince learns from the fox in Antoine de Saint Exupéry's enchanting fable *The Little Prince*. "And now here is my secret, a very simple secret," says the fox to the prince. "It is only with the heart that one can see rightly; what is essential is invisible to the eye."

One of the ways we can consciously cultivate gratitude and begin seeing with the heart is to look for opportunities to appreciate others—to show them how grateful we are for them. When we appreciate others, we share in their blessings. "Appreciation is a wonderful thing," Voltaire said. "It makes what is excellent in others belong to us as well."

Cultivating gratitude is learning to treat each other as we so often treat children, cherishing their every effort and cheering them on. No matter how crude a child's offering, it is always pure. It doesn't matter what they've drawn or what they've made, their work is beautiful and they need us to appreciate their effort. When a child sees that we are grateful for that effort, he or she will make another effort and then another. When someone is sincerely grateful for something you've done, doesn't it make all the difference? Doesn't it make you want to do it again and again?

Not only is gratitude and appreciation empowering, but it is healthy. Researchers at the Institute of HeartMath have shown that emotions like anger and frustration put a strain on the heart and other organs. Emotions like love, compassion and appreciation, on the other hand, have been shown to create harmony in the body, leading to enhanced immunity and improved hormonal balance.

"Scientists discovered a dramatic demonstration of love's transforming power when they looked at the difference between the effects of love and frustration," write David McArthur and Bruce McArthur. Frustration creates a chaotic pattern in our heart rate variability, which is the speeding up and slowing down of our heart rate. In contrast, they say, a deep heartfelt feeling of sincere appreciation produces a balanced, ordered pattern that is generally associated with efficient cardiovascular function. "It is a dynamic example of the transforming power of love operating at the level of our physical bodies," say the authors. "When this pattern is present in the heart, other systems in the body are strongly affected by its order and efficiency." [11]

Gratitude is so powerful that it can raise up or bring down an entire civilization. We can talk about everything that brought down the world's great civilizations, even as far back as the lost continent of Atlantis, but it all boils down to the failure to give gratitude to the Spirit. Civilizations fall when they fail to appreciate the gifts that God has given them.

> *If the only prayer you say in your whole life is "thank you," that would suffice.*
>
> —MEISTER ECKHART

When we are grateful for something, we acknowledge the giver, we take care of the gift we have been given and we share it with others. We realize that the true measure of success is not what we have achieved but whether or not we have used our God-given talents to bring out the best in others.

When we have gratitude, we want to give more because our cup is overflowing. Audrey Hepburn was a beautiful example of gratitude. In 1988 she became a Goodwill Ambassador for the United Nations International Children's Emergency Fund

(UNICEF). She could have enjoyed the last years of her life in a comfortable retirement. Instead, she spent her time climbing in and out of tiny airplanes that carried her to Ethiopia, Central America, Bangladesh, Vietnam and Somalia, where she witnessed firsthand the heartrending plight of the children. "I've been auditioning my whole life for this role, and I finally got it," she once said.

The actress felt compelled to do this out of gratitude for the food and relief she received as a child after World War II. "I've been terribly privileged, and it's logic that somebody who is privileged should do something for those who are not," she said. "They can't help themselves. They can't speak up for themselves, so we must."

HEART PERSPECTIVES

• **Look for opportunities to show your gratitude.** Ask yourself: Who can I appreciate today? How can I appreciate them?

• **Create a gratitude ritual.** As part of your daily spiritual practice, remember to thank God each day for a blessing in your life. Go into your heart and send your love and gratitude to God. Feel the return current over the figure-eight flow from your heart to God's heart.

• **Create a gratitude folder or journal.** Sometimes we don't recognize the gifts and good qualities we have. We tend to belittle ourselves. One way to remedy this is to keep a folder or journal where you specifically note your spiritual successes—the times when you expressed your higher nature.

If someone thanks you for something special that you did for them, or you finally manage to reprogram your inner software not to react when someone pushes your buttons, or you make a real difference in someone's life, make a note of it. As you make that note, thank God for giving you a gift that you could pass on to others. If you are feeling depressed or are tempted to get down on yourself, open your folder and read.

 # How Can I Love When...

For one human being to love another:
that is perhaps the most difficult of all our tasks,
the ultimate, the last test and proof, the work for which
all other work is but preparation.   —*RAINER MARIA RILKE*

Joyce is the dependable one in the family. When any of her brothers, sisters or cousins is going through a hard time, they know she will take them under her wing. Some of her relatives claim she's too naïve. They say she gives things away for free and that it's ridiculous the way she lets others take advantage of her. But Joyce doesn't live by their philosophy of life. When she gives, she isn't looking for a fair trade. She gives because that's what a loving heart would do.

Albert Schweitzer once said, "One thing I know: the only ones among you who will be really happy are those who will have sought and found how to serve." A heart that is open and empowered doesn't say, "I will do this nice thing or I will love this person so I can get something in return." In fact, if we do something with that motive in mind, then that something isn't love.

Love and self-interest simply don't mix.

During an interview at the turn of the new millennium, Nobel laureate novelist Saul Bellow observed that although we live in a society that "drills us continually in self-interest" and where sex "has become a substitute for love," people are fortunately still capable of discovering the unlimited generosity of love. "You see very peculiar effects of generosity upon a human system," he said. "There is nothing you would not share willingly, gladly, for the sake of the love that you bear another person—and this is in a society that... equates self-interest with sanity and sacrifice with utopianism or utter madness."[12]

Mother Teresa, whose entire life was an exercise in love, did not minister to the poor and homeless with an ulterior motive in mind, not even with the goal of converting the poor. As she once said, "Conversion is not our work—that is the work of God. We never ask anyone to change their religion. Our mission is to reveal God by doing our service."

We all reveal a little bit of the divine when we touch someone's life personally through an act of love. What Mother Teresa knew is that many people cannot experience God's comfort or wisdom or love unless we *personally* bring it to them. That is the great master key that the mystics of the world have discovered.

They have also discovered that the mature heart doesn't evaluate the object of its love before sharing that love. During a question-and-answer session, someone attending one of my workshops told me that he was in love with his wife but he was having trouble loving her or anyone unconditionally. "It seems like I'm always putting a condition on that love," he said. Then he asked how he could begin to break down the barriers to his expression of love.

The young man's question was a good one. How can we love when the other person is irritable, selfish or depressed—behaviors that we, of course, never exhibit! Yet when someone is irritable, selfish or depressed, isn't that exactly when she needs our heart the most? As someone keenly observed, "People need loving the most when they deserve it the least."

When we truly love, we maintain an awareness of the potential of the individual to become who he or she really is—whether it's our spouse, a co-worker, our children or even ourselves. We don't have to love people's naughty deeds, but we can love the soul that is still struggling, as we all are, to become a greater expression of the Spirit.

God knows about our mistakes and he still loves us. Even in our darkest hours, he sees our great spiritual potential. If we are to create an alchemy of the heart, a transformation and evolution of the heart, that's what we need to do too. If we can view situations from God's perspective, we can begin to love as God loves—and, after all, isn't that the goal?

> *Expecting something in return leads to a scheming mind. So an ancient once said, "Throw false spirituality away like a pair of old shoes."*
>
> —KYONG HO

When you get into a difficult situation, try asking God to show you how he loves. I did this one day. I was meditating in my heart on God's love and I asked God to enter my heart so that I could understand how to love as God would love. I was blessed with the miracle of feeling God loving life through my heart. And I realized that as great as our expression of love might be, there is a big difference between divine love and human love. There is a big difference between the way we see and the way God sees.

Thomas Merton had a glimpse of this. He wrote, "Then it was as if I suddenly saw the secret beauty of their hearts, . . . the person that each one is in God's eyes. If only they could see themselves as they really are. If only we could see each other that way, there would be no more need for war or hatred, no more need for cruelty or greed."

The great luminaries of the Spirit call this the science of the immaculate concept—holding in mind the pure image of the soul's divine blueprint. For our souls were created in the image and likeness of the Divine. The science of the immaculate concept is like the science of visualization used by peak performers and exceptional athletes. Studies show that when they visualize themselves meeting their targets, they are much more likely to do just that.

If we can visualize ourselves and others reaching our highest potential, if we can treat others as if they are already acting in loving ways, we will compel that highest outcome to manifest. The more we *see* each other as masterful beings, the more likely we are to *become* masterful beings.

In the sixteenth century, Kabbalist Moses Cordovero wrote a popular and practical handbook for cultivating spiritual virtues, *The Palm Tree of Deborah*. His premise is that since we were made in the image and likeness of God, we are meant to imitate our Creator through our virtues and deeds.

Cordovero begins by explaining how we can cultivate the attribute of mercy by holding in mind the highest image for others. When people offend or provoke us, he advises, think about their good qualities. If we have trouble doing this, he suggests that we recall, as God does, the good deeds they have done from the day of their birth. When people seem unworthy, he says, remember that there was a time, even if it was in their infancy, when they did not sin.

Holding the immaculate concept for others doesn't mean, however, that we should ignore the warnings of our heart and soul when we sense real physical, mental or emotional danger. We don't have to condone an individual's deeds or allow him to harm us. Although love does not judge, it is discriminating. Although love does not harm, it is truthful.

Sometimes the highest love is truth, especially when those we love need a wake-up call. If you cannot support what someone is doing, you can quietly but firmly say, "This is not something I can join you in or go along with, and this is not something I can allow you to do in my presence."

Our relationships form some of the most important stepping-stones for our path of spiritual evolution. If someone has a hardcore pattern of descending to depths of consciousness that are unacceptable to you and they are not willing to work on healing those patterns, then your progress can be held back. That is why it is said that in a marriage we should be equally yoked.

On the other hand, we can't just withdraw our support because one minute our partner, friend or child does something we don't like. If we try to love as God loves, we will champion the right of each person to walk his own path and realize his full divine potential without heckling, henpecking or judging. We will find ways to create a mutual support system of the heart.

Researchers have found that strong heart-ties are not only emotionally supportive but they can keep us physically alive and well. For example, in the early sixties researchers studied Roseto, a small town in Pennsylvania established by Italian immigrants in the 1880s. The citizens of Roseto were much healthier than those in nearby towns. They had low rates of senility and their rate of death from heart attacks was 40 percent less than their neighbors. Yet the Rosetans were not significantly different from their neighbors in factors like obesity, smoking, lack of exercise and serum cholesterol levels. What was different was their level of community and connectedness.

> *Love is not love / Which alters when it alteration finds, ... / O no, it is an ever fixèd mark / That looks on tempests and is never shaken.*
>
> —WILLIAM SHAKESPEARE

Dr. Stewart Wolf, one of the researchers who studied this phenomenon, dubbed the Roseto Effect, said that the single biggest factor contributing to their good health was "a remarkable cohesiveness and sense of unconditional support within the community." At that time, their houses were close together and many of them lived in three-generation households.

Other researchers noted that the Rosetans distinguished themselves by their enjoyment of life and their mutual trust and support. No one felt abandoned. What's more, later studies showed that as the younger citizens of Roseto assumed a more

Americanized, isolated lifestyle and the town's strong social ties began to loosen, the rate of heart attacks rose to match the rest of the country.

The Roseto Effect has important implications for how we treat our elderly and incorporate them into our communities. More than that, it shows us that the bonds of the heart are essential to our very existence. Other studies have confirmed these findings. One study showed that advanced breast cancer patients who participate in a support group live twice as long as those who don't. Another study from Duke University showed that those with heart disease who are married or who have a confidant live longer. As French actress Jeanne Moreau once said, "Age does not protect you from love but love to some extent protects you from age."

HEART PERSPECTIVES

• **Hold the "immaculate concept" for yourself and others.** Do you feel that you put unrealistic conditions on your love in any of your relationships? When you find it difficult to give full support and love to another, remind yourself how patient God has been with you and how much God loves the soul of the one who is troubling you. Try to look beyond the outer personality to the soul's true identity and potential. Fix your vision on that highest image, let your love flow and let God take care of the rest.

• **Assess your support network.** Have there been times in your life when a lack of close ties with others has affected your well being—body, mind or soul? Today is there one or more people with whom you share a close bond of mutual trust and support? If not, consider joining in an activity with others who share your goals, such as a group that meets to discuss books, that mentors children, or that works to change the conditions in your neighborhood.

PART THREE

HEALING
the Heart

*Healing the heart begins with mercy—
extending mercy to others, extending mercy
to ourselves. It begins with affirming that we are
in control of our destiny. No matter what we have
done, no matter what we have experienced, we can
transcend ourselves. We can learn to master the
creative flow of energy through our heart.*

The Merciful Heart

Happiness is good health and a bad memory.
—*INGRID BERGMAN*

It had been twenty years since Rich divorced his first wife, but he still felt badly about the way that marriage had ended. "I was totally involved in myself and I was confused about so many issues," he remembers. He also regretted that he had never expressed to his in-laws from that marriage how much he valued them and how sorry he was that the divorce had to impact their lives so powerfully.

After many years he mustered the courage to write to his ex-wife asking for forgiveness. He sent the letter to his son from that marriage and asked him to deliver it to his mother.

"The next thing I knew, she was calling me on the phone," says Rich. "When I heard her words of understanding, it was as if someone had just opened my heart for the first time. She also had a message from her mother: 'Please tell Rich that I forgave him so long ago I've almost forgotten it.'

To me that was the kindest thing a human being could say to another human being. For years I'd been dealing with all sorts of guilt and those words healed me."

Opening his heart and laying bare his innermost feelings in that letter was a huge step for Rich. He had to overcome his fear of being rejected. But once he acted—once he extended mercy and asked for mercy—the fear and guilt were washed away by the healing power of love. Just how much courage it took came home to him when he recounted the story to his cousin, who had recently gone through a difficult divorce himself. "When I encouraged him to seek resolution because it had meant so much to me, he absolutely panicked. He couldn't get away from my desk fast enough," says Rich.

That's our normal reaction. When something is difficult or distasteful, we want to flee as far and as fast as we can. Winston Churchill once said, "Men occasionally stumble over the truth, but most of them pick themselves up and hurry off as if nothing had happened." When we're on a path of the heart and we "stumble" over a situation that needs resolution, no matter how uncomfortable it may be, we don't just pick ourselves up and hurry off. For we know that we are not really free to make spiritual progress unless we stop and apply mercy. First, last and always, we are called to forgive, forgive and forgive.

There is a simple law behind that injunction. When we refuse to forgive someone who has wronged us, even if he wrongs us again and again, we tie ourselves to that person. "All you are unable to give," said André Gide, "possesses you." The person we refuse to forgive, the person we are angry with, becomes our master. No matter how hard we try to move

> *Love and you shall be loved. All love is mathematically just, as much as the two sides of an algebraic equation.*
> —RALPH WALDO EMERSON

in any direction, we can only go as far as the rope of nonresolution allows us to—and it's usually a very short rope. The rope is short because our soul inevitably gravitates back to the scene to restore harmony and reach resolution.

That's why people who go to their graves without making peace with their adversaries will be in for a surprise when they reach the other side. They will find out that when we don't let go of our resentment, anger or desire for revenge, we have to reincarnate with the same people again and again until we learn to love. Thus deep-seated vendettas between families and even nations are not just generations old; they can go back centuries or even lifetimes. The feuding goes on with no end in sight until they forgive.

Not only do people carry nonforgiveness to their graves, but they may go to their graves more quickly if they do not forgive. A University of Tennessee study measured the effect of a forgiving personality. Researchers measured indicators like blood pressure, forehead muscle tension and heart rate as students spoke about experiences of betrayal. The researchers found that those who forgave more easily had lower blood pressure and a smaller increase in blood pressure than those who held grudges.[1]

The issue of forgiveness is confusing to many of us because we have been erroneously taught that forgiveness wipes away the transgression or the crime. We think that when we ask for forgiveness for something we have done or when we forgive another, that's the end of the matter and we have no further responsibility. But forgiveness does not equal absolution. We are still required to take full responsibility for our actions. If you pay some-one to paint your car blue and he paints it red, you can forgive him but he still has to rectify the situa-tion and repaint your car.

When God forgives us, our negative karma (or sin) is sealed for a time. It's as if God takes this bundle of karma off our back so we have time to pursue the path of self-mastery and prepare to pass the exam when it comes around again. And it will come again. When we do finally pass the test, we can graduate to the next level of spiritual mastery.

That's how the universe works. If we lose our temper or get angry, we will be tested again on the formula of patience and forgiveness. The test may come in a new set of circumstances or it may come as a replay of the same scenario with the same actors. Whatever the case, we will have to show how much love and forgiveness we can infuse into the situation to heal ourselves and others.

Jesus was a prophet of love, and one of the most profound things he ever taught about the spiritual dynamics of love is in the Lord's Prayer: "Forgive us our debts as we forgive our debtors." We're so used to hearing those words that we don't really think about what they mean: Forgive us our own faults and mistakes *in the same manner as* we forgive the faults and mistakes of others.

That's the fundamental law of karma: As you do unto others, so it will be done unto you. God will extend forgiveness to us in the same proportion that we extend our heart's mercy to others. And if we do not forgive, then mercy will be withheld from us. Thus the biggest danger of the unmerciful heart is that it hurts the one who retains it.

> The story of a love is not important—what is important is that one is capable of love.
>
> —HELEN HAYES

The law of forgiveness is a simple equation of energy, for whatever we think, feel and do has ramifications at energetic levels of our being. The ancient Oriental art of feng shui, for example, says that clutter or blockages within our environment can create blockages in our life. The same thing applies to our internal terrain. When we freely give and receive love, when we quickly deal with and resolve issues that come into our lives, energy can move. But if we hold on to resentment or anger, energy gets blocked up. When a lack of forgiveness and love becomes acute, the blocked energy hardens around the heart.

At spiritual levels this creates hardness of heart.

If you want to heal the heart and activate mercy, a good rule of thumb is to handle that unpleasant, sticky issue that just walked into your life as fast as you can. Forgive others and ask for forgiveness with all the sincerity of your heart so that both of you can move forward.

The great adepts did not say, however, that forgiveness was necessarily easy. It's not always easy to forgive those who have committed grave crimes against body, mind and soul. A woman once poured out her heart to me in a letter and said: "Try as hard as I can, I cannot forgive my former husband for molesting my daughters. They have suffered all their lives as a result of this. They have problems in their marriages. They have not been able to work through the trauma of it all and I cannot forgive him. What shall I do?"

I prayed to God about this and I received an empowering and liberating teaching, which I passed on to this woman. Resolution, I learned, is a two-step process. The first step is to invoke divine mercy. We can forgive the soul of the one who committed the wrong and we can ask God to forgive the soul.

The second step is to invoke divine justice for the

binding of the negative forces, within and without, that hold the soul in their grip and work through that soul. We can ask God to restrain the unreal self, the dark side of the person that caused him or her to commit the wrong. We can also ask God to give the soul an opportunity to repent of his deeds and an opportunity to strengthen himself so he can resist the urge to do wrong when it knocks again at his door.

However, just because we forgive someone, it doesn't mean we condone his harmful actions. But it does mean we can let go of our sense of injustice and let God take care of the situation. The when, where and how is God's business—"Vengeance is mine; I will repay, saith the Lord."

That means it's our work to forgive, and it's God's work to render judgment and deliver the increments of karma that will help the soul learn her lessons. In fact, we can love the spiritual nature that resides deep within each person no matter what his actions are. The animating fire at the very core of our cells is God, and therefore we can love the soul and honor that light even if the consciousness that uses that light is no longer serving the Spirit.

The understanding of these two components of forgiveness—forgiving the soul and asking God to bind the negative forces working through the soul—was the healing of a lifetime to the woman who wrote me the letter. It freed her, because she knew that God would dispense both divine mercy and divine justice. After years of anguish, she could at last let go of the situation.

HEART PERSPECTIVES

• **Self-reflect about your capacity to forgive.** When issues come up, are you able to easily resolve them or do you carry them around with you for a long time? Are you able to let go, turn them over to God and forget about them?

• **Seek resolution.** Is there a situation in your life that you have never fully resolved—something that may have happened years ago that still burdens you at times?

If there is someone you haven't forgiven or who hasn't forgiven you, talk to him or her or write a letter. Ask for forgiveness and/or tell him you forgive him. If the person has passed on, you can write this in a letter, burn it and ask the angels to deliver your letter to that soul.

The Mystery of Self-Transcendence

As human beings, our greatness lies not so
much in being able to remake the world...
as in being able to remake ourselves.   —MAHATMA GANDHI

Frequently the most important person you
have to forgive is yourself. Sometimes we
believe we aren't worthy of that forgiveness. We
look at the human part of ourselves and we say we
just aren't good enough. But we aren't here to perfect the human part of ourselves. We're here to
liberate our own inner greatness and manifest the
full potential of our spiritual self.

Every one of us has made mistakes, and it is
necessary to contact the pain we may have caused
others. It is necessary to feel, with the full sensitivity of our heart, the remorse that convinces our
soul never to hurt another part of life like that
again. But it is also necessary to get over it.

No matter what mistakes we've made, we
were doing the best we could at the time. Now it's
time to forgive ourselves, to get on with our life
and to keep our eye focused on the vast spiritual

potential we have inside of us. We all have that potential, but we haven't always accepted it.

One of the reasons self-forgiveness and self-acceptance can be so hard is that many of us were belittled or ridiculed when we were growing up. Our accusers may have been relentless in their condemnation. The Book of Revelation, which is a drama of archetypes, talks about the accuser of our brethren who "accused them before our God day and night." The accuser of the brethren is the archetype of those who make it a habit to criticize and condemn others.

In the face of such accusers, we erroneously come to believe that we just aren't lovable. When those barbs of criticism are flying, what we don't always realize is that the accusers must criticize and carp and put us down in order to feel good about themselves.

We can certainly benefit from constructive and uplifting feedback, but all too often our society reinforces the negatives. We tend to look at people and mentally take them apart. We don't like what they're wearing or the way their eyebrows go or the shape of their glasses. We have been taught to examine each other (and ourselves) against impossible standards instead of using the great gift of vision to behold the living Spirit in each other and to honor that Spirit. We have been taught that in order to be accepted and loved we must live up to those outer standards. Yet the real longing of our soul is to be loved for who and what we are at our core, not for our personality or appearance or even our accomplishments.

> *It's not my job to motivate players.... It's my job not to demotivate them.*
>
> —LOU HOLTZ

I remember one day, as I was walking down the street with my husband, Mark, how he conveyed his love for me—the real me. He said, "Elizabeth, I love your soul." I can remember how I wept. For the first time in my life I had met someone who had the capacity to know my soul—as well as all my faults, my mistakes, my problems—and who could love me just the way I was. He loved me not because I was perfect or imperfect, but because I was me.

Each time we criticize, we actually crucify the God in each other. On the path of the heart, we have a duty to take that God down from the cross by nurturing rather than tearing down. If you are tempted to criticize, take a moment to stop and examine what really bothers you. Ask yourself, why do I need to criticize, and what am I afraid of?

Psychologists tell us that criticism of others is actually a criticism of some part of ourselves. What we most dislike in another is related to a trait we don't like in ourselves. Dr. Harville Hendrix says that he and his wife discovered this in their relationship. "We had to learn to love in the other person the trait we most disliked in ourselves," he says.

For example, Hendrix says he tends to get annoyed when his wife spends too much time on the telephone. Yet he sometimes spends too much time on the computer. He says that if he can understand why talking on the phone is valuable to his wife and if he can honor her needs, he can also bypass his own unconscious hatred of some part of himself. He increases not only his love for his wife, but also his love for himself. Every time we refrain from judging others and approach them with empathy rather than judgment, he says, we will also be honoring rather than rejecting ourselves.[2]

The very important implication of this is that many of the psychological, spiritual and even physical challenges we face may begin with nonforgiveness and nonacceptance of ourselves. When we don't forgive ourselves, we tend not to forgive others. When we hold impossible standards for ourselves, we tend to do the same for others. When we are harsh and rigid with ourselves, we tend to be harsh and rigid with others. But when we are at peace with ourselves, we can meet the world with peace. When we forgive ourselves, we can more easily forgive others.

The truth of the matter is that when God gave us free will and set us in this dense, physical world, he knew we would make mistakes. Trial and error is the way of the eternal alchemist, the one who experiments again and again in pursuit of a higher goal. A mistake is intended to propel us upward and onward as we learn from and celebrate the lesson that has allowed us to grow. Of course, we were never meant to remain on a treadmill, going around in circles and repeating the same mistakes instead of rising higher and higher on a spiral of self-transcendence.

> *All life is an experiment.*
> —RALPH WALDO EMERSON

Self-transcendence is the law of the universe. The spiritual world, like the physical universe, is not static. The beings who inhabit spiritual realms, from the saints and masters to the mighty arch-angels, are continually growing, progressing and maturing in love, wisdom and power. With the energy we have at our disposal every day, the energy that drives the engine of our life, we too are meant to continually transcend ourselves.

When we don't experience progress, it's because we are stuck in a self-limiting matrix. We can't conceive of the higher matrix of what we could be. If today you hold the same image of yourself that you held yesterday, then with today's energy you are creating the same patterns that you were creating yesterday. If you have a belief lurking anywhere in your being that accepts limitation, that accepts the condemnation of the acerbic accusers, it will prevent you from being re-created in the likeness and image of that higher pattern. And when you criticize others, you are encouraging them to hold on to a limiting concept of themselves also.

Simply put, if we are not what we want to be, it could be because too much of our energy is invested in the old pattern. *But love creates the new matrix.* Love is self-transcending and love shows us that we are in control of our destiny.

I can be a new person every day—that's an exciting concept. You are a co-creator with Spirit, and the co-creative process is happening right where you are. You are a scientist of the Spirit. You are an alchemist in the laboratory of being. What you create every day can be a new expression of love if you want it to be.

HEART PERSPECTIVES

• Are you holding on to a self-limiting matrix of yourself? What are the erroneous beliefs you may hold about yourself that have been reinforced by misguided authority figures, peers, et cetera? What is the higher image that you would like to manifest? What could you do to help yourself sustain that higher image day by day?

• The next time you feel condemned, give yourself permission to affirm: *"I have called upon the law of forgiveness. My God has forgiven me. I am going forth to do better today. And therefore I do not accept this guilt, this shame or this label of sinner!"* Throw all of your blame, shame and sense of guilt into the alchemical fires of the heart. Let those fires, like a great furnace of forgiveness, burn up the prison bars around your heart and set your soul free.

• **Use circumstances as a mirror.** Think of a trait or behavior in another person that bothers you. Does it remind you of something you don't like about yourself? Put yourself in the other person's shoes and try to understand why he or she may need to act that way. Now think about the parallel behavior within yourself and ask yourself how that behavior serves a purpose for you.

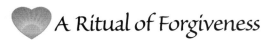 # A Ritual of Forgiveness

He who cannot forgive others destroys the bridge
over which he himself must pass.   *—GEORGE HERBERT*

When we don't process issues as they arrive at our doorstep, the energy of nonresolution can build up, like layers of sedimentary rock, blocking the doors of the heart. It can keep us tossing and turning in bed all night long. And when our buttons get pushed, our unresolved feelings can suddenly awaken, causing us to react in ways that often surprise us.

A good way to keep the channels of the heart open is to create your own surrender ritual at the end of each day before you go to sleep (see page 106). As part of that ritual, you can ask God to show you the practical steps to take the next day to move toward resolution.

A universal prayer that has become a successful part of many people's surrender ritual is the Affirmation for Forgiveness. A friend gave John a copy of this affirmation and he tucked it into his desk drawer at work. That week he went out to lunch with a friend of his wife's. She had some bad news. She told John that his wife was having an affair with a vice president of the sales division where both he and his wife worked, and that it had been going on even before they were married.

Upset and hurt, John called his wife and then her lover to confront them. "When I hung up the phone," he remembers, "I could feel this burning rage overwhelming me. It would have been easy to lose control and do something stupid. Suddenly I felt a very clear prompting to open the desk drawer, take out the forgiveness affirmation and give it. I said it aloud several times. I gave it quietly, because I was at work, but with all of my heart. As I did, I felt an incredible presence of peace come over me. I felt the volatile energy dissipate. I was able to think clearly."

As he calmed down, John remembered that his wife's father had been an alcoholic and she had never felt loved by her father. Now she was doing the best she could and was trying to please both John and her lover. The incident also confirmed what John had been suspecting for months—that for his own spiritual growth it was time to move beyond this relationship.

Instead of getting caught up in a game of revenge or guilt, John took what in this case was a positive step for both himself and his wife. Within a matter of weeks they were divorced. Because he had forgiven his wife, he was free to move on. "We actually ended up parting as friends," says John. "Giving that affirmation helped me release the anger and resolve an unhealthy situation that was holding me back spiritually."

HEART PERSPECTIVES

• **Create your own surrender ritual.** Just before you fall asleep, let the day's events pass before your inner eye like a movie. Then speak to God about your day. If you are burdened by unresolved circumstances, ask God to forgive you, to help you forgive others and to reestablish a figure-eight flow of love between you and those you name. Send love over this figure-eight from your heart to the hearts of all whom you have ever wronged and all who have ever wronged you.

Ask God or your favorite saint, master or angel to tutor your soul while you sleep and show you specifically how to resolve the situation the next day. Ask for the opportunity at the right place and the right time to set things right.

• **Experiment with the Affirmation for Forgiveness.** Before you give this affirmation, ask for forgiveness for yourself and for those you will name. In your mind's eye, see a sacred fire blazing within your heart. See this fire of love as an intense pink flame mixed with violet.[3] See these flames of forgiveness becoming more and more intense as they transmute at energetic levels the calcified energy of nonforgiveness and the memories of hurt and pain.

Your heart can be an instrument of divine love as you give this affirmation. As you say the words, send the violet-pink flames from your heart to the hearts of those you have named. See these flames soften and then melt down all hardness of heart.

As you become more adept at this visualization, you can send flaming spheres of light to more and more people, even visualizing the flames of forgiveness over entire cities, countries or war-torn areas as a healing unguent of forgiveness. Repeat the affirmation below as many times as you like. The more you repeat it, the greater the momentum and power you will build.

AFFIRMATION FOR FORGIVENESS

> *I AM* forgiveness acting here,*
> *Casting out all doubt and fear,*
> *Setting men forever free*
> *With wings of cosmic victory.*
>
> *I AM calling in full power*
> *For forgiveness every hour;*
> *To all life in every place*
> *I flood forth forgiving grace.*

---

*Each time you say, "I AM" (from "I AM THAT I AM"), you are really saying, "God in me is. . . . " The "I AM" is the power of Spirit working personally through you.

♥ Making Peace with God

The mark of your ignorance is the depth of your belief
in injustice and tragedy. What the caterpillar calls the
end of the world, the Master calls the butterfly.

—RICHARD BACH

"I just don't understand. How could God
have let this happen? How could he let
my baby (or husband or sister or mother) die?"

That's the way we are tempted to respond
when we hear about tragedies for which there is no
logical explanation. But it's not God who "lets"
these tragedies happen. The law of the circle, or the
law of karma ("what goes around comes around"),
tells us that what happens to us in the present is the
result of causes we ourselves have set in motion in
the past—in this life or past lives. Out of his love
for our souls, God gave us free will and he respects
that free will. He allows us to experiment and
therefore to learn by direct experience the consequences of our actions.

Of course, people initiate original acts of negative karma every day when they harm others.
Thus, everything that happens is not necessarily

the payback for something we have done in the past. Sometimes souls even volunteer to make sacrifices to help someone close to them learn an important soul lesson.

We can never know for sure the real reason behind any tragedy. But we always have a choice. We can curse God and/or blame ourselves or others, or we can open our heart, send out more love and try to understand the lesson meant for our soul.

We don't always consciously know when we are angry at God. Sometimes we can only tell by the symptoms that emerge out of the sublevels of our being. Unconscious anger, for instance, can make us spend an inordinate amount of time eating or sleeping. It can make us passive, resentful or disinterested as a form of silent rebellion. Unconscious anger can lead us to criticize others or fixate on things outside of ourselves, even our work, to avoid facing the roots of our anger—anything to escape from reality.

If we never resolve the hurt that usually lies just beneath the anger, we will carry that anger and that hurt with us our whole life. In the long run, conscious or unconscious anger at God can affect the set of our sails perhaps for lifetimes to come.

Sometimes the only way to deal with our sorrow (and perhaps this is the lesson we are meant to learn) is to be grateful for what we do have. During the devastating fires that swept through Los Alamos, a television reporter asked one of the residents how he felt when he saw the pictures of the flames consuming his hometown and his home. "When we saw those pictures," the man said, "my wife and I just hugged each other and told each other how grateful we were for what we do have."

> *It has done me good to be somewhat parched by the heat and drenched by the rain of life.*
> —HENRY WADSWORTH LONGFELLOW

John and Reve Walsh met the ultimate test when their six-year-old son, Adam, was abducted at a store in Florida while his mother was shopping just three aisles away. After weeks, Adam's severed head was found in a canal. John, then a hotel developer, was devastated. He couldn't work and he lost everything. But he and his wife shaped their grief and loss of their child into something that could save millions.

The work of John and Reve led to the passage of two bills, one of which founded the National

Center for Missing and Exploited Children with its toll-free hotline. They also founded the nonprofit Adam Walsh Child Resource Center, which is dedicated to legislative reform. In addition, John became host of *America's Most Wanted,* the most popular crime-fighting program on television.

The Walsh family's tragedy also resulted in the Code Adam program implemented in some stores. Code Adam is a special alert announced over the public address system when a child is reported missing. The salespeople stop to look for the missing child and monitor all exits to prevent the child from being abducted.

John has received numerous awards and has been honored by three presidents for his outstanding efforts to help missing and exploited children. "You're not supposed to bury your children," he told a *People* magazine reporter. "They're your legacy. But I would never have accomplished the things I have, such as the Missing Children's Act, which brings the FBI immediately into cases involving missing children, if it wasn't for Adam and my love for him."[4]

Although we may not have to face situations as tragic as Adam's death, we all face trying circumstances. Will we become angry or will we try to find the hidden blessing or lesson? The Taoist philosopher Lieh Tze illustrated this point in his story about a poor old man who lived with his son. One day when the man's horse disappeared, his neighbors came by to tell him how sorry they were.

"Why do you assume this is a problem?" the man asked. Some time later, the horse returned, accompanied by several other wild horses. When the neighbors congratulated the old man on the sudden multiplication of his assets, he said, "Why do you think this is good luck?"

As it turned out, with all the horses around, his son started riding and consequently broke his leg. When the neighbors all gathered to say how sorry they were at this new calamity, the man asked, "What makes you think this is a misfortune?" Following this, war broke out and his still-lame son was declared exempt and did not have to go off to war. The old man could have become enraged with each of the seemingly negative turn of events and shaken his fist at God. But he surrendered each circumstance and watched for the hidden blessing to appear.

HEART PERSPECTIVES

• Reflect on a difficult situation in your life or another's. Look deep within and ask yourself if you are still harboring any anger. Can you find a hidden blessing or lesson in that situation? How can you shape your loss into something positive that can help others?

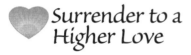 # Surrender to a Higher Love

Love like you've never been hurt.
Dance like nobody's watching.   *—SATCHEL PAIGE*

At one time or another we've all felt like Charlie Brown when he said, "Nothing takes the taste out of peanut butter quite like unrequited love." Perhaps a relationship or a friendship didn't work out and we feel abandoned or rejected. Or we loved someone only to realize that they weren't what we thought they were. Sometimes the sorrow or the guilt is almost unbearable. We gave so much of our heart—for what?

Sometimes the answer, the "for what," is in the

pain itself. "Your pain," wrote Kahlil Gibran, "is the breaking of the shell that encloses your understanding." When you are in pain because your love has been rejected, you can ask God to heal the hurt, to bless the one you have loved and to help both of you become more of your true self. Most of all, you can ask God to show you *why* you are hurting.

Maybe we hurt because we expected something unrealistic in return for our love or we expected others to fill in the blanks in our own self-esteem—a job that only we can do by loving and nurturing ourselves. Maybe we were leaning on the human personality rather than seeking the spiritual essence that lies beyond the personality. Whatever the source of the pain, if we pay attention to it, it can teach us.

> Love is never lost.
> If not reciprocated, it will flow back and soften and purify the heart."
> —WASHINGTON IRVING

The most important thing to remember is that no love is ever wasted. "There is no unreturn'd love," wrote Walt Whitman, "the pay is certain one way or another." No matter what happens, love is always worthwhile because every moment of loving brings us closer to the higher love our souls are seeking. At the most fundamental level of our being, we are yearning to reunite with our divine lovers—God and our "twin flame." Our twin flame is our "other half," as Plato described it, our original partner who was created with us in the beginning.*

Twin flames have often been lured away from each other and temporarily detoured en route to their divine destiny together. These sidetracks have snared us into circumstances where we have created negative karma with others. In many cases, we aren't free to be with our twin flame until we first balance these karmic debts with others. The only thing that will free us from these karmic entanglements is love.

So every morsel of love we give not only helps us balance our karmic debts, but it also brings us that much closer to reunion with our twin flame and with God. Realizing that love can help balance the debts we owe others has helped me see all kinds of

---

*Some use the word *soul mate* to refer to *twin flame*, but the terms have different meanings. Twin flames are two halves of the Divine Whole. They are souls who have the same spiritual origin and unique pattern of identity. Soul mates share a complementary calling in life and are partners for the journey. You may have more than one soul mate but you have only one twin flame. See *Soul Mates and Twin Flames: The Spiritual Dimension of Love and Relationships* published by Summit University Press.

relationships as learning experiences and opportunities to give more love, even if that love seemed to be rejected.

Another way to look at our initiations of love is through the lens of bhakti yoga. In Hinduism, one of the four yogas (or paths to union with God) is bhakti, the yoga of divine love. Bhakti yoga is practiced in different ways, but at its essence it is devotion to God above all else—a devotion that leads to the heart of God.

Whenever we reach out to touch another, we are really sending the arrow of our love from our heart to God's heart. When we serve another—whether it's the confused child, the cranky co-worker or the eccentric elderly woman we help up the elevator—we are serving the God who lives within that one. In essence, we are surrendering to a higher love.

If we practice seeing beyond the outer personality of the one we are serving to the real goal of our love (God), we will realize that our love for anyone and everyone is really a reflection of our love for God. After all, it was God who we were in love with from the beginning to the ending. Not only that, but when we love, it is God who is loving through us.

Each one of us wears a mask, in a sense, and behind the mask is the living presence of the Spirit. God disguises himself so that we have many, many opportunities to give our love back to him by loving all these different manifestations and expressions of the Spirit. The mask itself may be seemingly imperfect, yet we know that the Lord of Love lives

> *Love the people with whom fate brings you together, but do so with all your heart.*
> —MARCUS AURELIUS

within. In reality, love comes from only one source, and we can be grateful that many people in our lives have been beautiful instruments of that divine love.

So when you feel a painful loss and you ask yourself, "I gave so much of my heart—for what?" ask yourself another question: *Who and what have I really loved?*

If you allow yourself to go deeply enough, the answer will be: *All the while I was really loving the Spirit who abides within that one.* The beauty and intensity of your love could not possibly have been the love for the outer self. In reality, you loved the soul and the spiritual essence expressing itself in and through that person. And that kind of love is never wasted. It is the love of God.

In her memoirs Alma Maria Mahler, wife of composer Gustav Mahler, spoke of this kind of deep inner love that they shared. "Each of us was jealous of the other, though we belied it," she wrote. "He often used to say: 'If you were suddenly disfigured by some illness, smallpox, for example, then at last, when you were pleasing in the sight of nobody else—then at last I could show how I loved you.'"[5]

HEART PERSPECTIVES

• **Reflect on your interpersonal relationships** with family, friends, mates, partners or co-workers. Can you recall a turning point in any of these relationships where once a "debt" was paid off through love and service to each other, both of you could move on?

• **Look beyond the pain.** When you are faced with rejection or the sorrow of what seems to be a lost love, ask yourself: Why have I loved? Who and what have I really loved? What is the message? What is the outworn "shell" of limited understanding that this pain is trying to break open? What is the new understanding that is being revealed to me?

- **Love the highest.** Try to realize that as you love another, as you serve another, you are really loving and serving the divine spirit who lives within that one. You are really sending the arrow of love from your heart to God's heart.

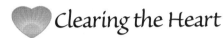 ## Clearing the Heart

When all the knots of the heart are unloosened,
then even here, in this human birth, the mortal
becomes immortal.   —*KATHA UPANISHAD*

Many people believe that the inclinations of the heart are always right. "Follow your heart," they say. Yet the heart, like any of our spiritual faculties, can become clouded, especially when we have not healed from past hurts or forgiven ourselves or others.

For instance, our heart's natural sensitivity and desire to open up and share could be eclipsed by fears of rejection. Painful memories of the past can cause us to be cautious or defensive rather than compassionate and supportive. When we encounter a difficult circumstance that we would rather not deal with, it's all too easy to retreat into our comfort zone behind our castle walls. Up go the defenses! But we have another choice. In addition to the techniques for forgiveness and self-transcendence we have offered in Part Three, another powerful way to heal the heart is to clear the heart.

Right now a crystal clear stream of energy is flowing from Spirit through your Higher Self to your heart. It's a transfer of energy from Above to below. It's moving with the speed of light and it bursts within your heart as a spiritual flame, beating your physical heart and sustaining the flow of life within you. That moving stream of energy is your natural resource of pure, creative love.

Moment by moment as that energy comes into your heart, you are deciding how to use it. What unique vibration are you going to imprint upon that energy? Will you express that energy as love or criticism, peace or anger, generosity or selfishness?

If I choose to radiate the energy flowing through my heart as love, this energy will eventually return to me as the blessings of love. If I send out anger, resentment or criticism, this discordant energy, by the law of the circle, will also return to me. Sometime, somewhere we will be on the receiving end of all that we have sent forth.

When the current of negative energy we have sent out returns to us, we have an opportunity to change its character—to turn it into something positive. As the law of conservation of energy tells us, energy is neither created nor destroyed. But it can go through stages of transformation and refinement. If we choose to meet hatred with hatred, anger with anger, fear with fear, the vicious circle will continue. If instead we meet hatred with love, anger with love, and fear with love, we turn the circle into a spiral, bringing everyone up to a new level. "Hatred never ceases by hatred but by love alone is healed," said the Buddha.

We've all misused the energies of our heart at one time or another. Maybe we've been unkind, critical or stingy. At energetic levels, our negative thoughts, feelings and actions create what looks like a molasses substance around the heart. In severe cases—when a heart is surfeited in anger, pride, resentment or selfishness—this negative energy collects and solidifies, like rock or concrete. This "hardness of heart" can prevent the sunlight of love from reaching our heart or radiating from it. This negative energy remains with us as part of our consciousness until we transmute it by love.

Just as we wash off the dirt and grime we pick up every day, so we can have a daily ritual of bathing and purifying our heart to free it of the debris that clouds our spiritual vision and makes us lose perspective. Each spiritual tradition has its particular practices for purification. Many of these are sacred formulas of prayer and meditation that call forth the light of the Holy Spirit to purify the heart. In some traditions, this powerfully transforming energy of the Holy Spirit has been seen as a violet light, known as the violet flame.

> When a mirror is covered with dust, it cannot reflect images. ... It is even the same with all beings. If their minds are not clear of stain, [God, the Absolute,] cannot reveal itself in them.
>
> —THE AWAKENING OF FAITH

Just as a ray of sunlight passing through a prism is refracted into the seven colors of the rainbow, so spiritual light manifests as seven rays, or flames. When we call forth these spiritual flames in our prayers and meditations, each flame creates a specific action in our body, mind and soul. The violet flame is the color and frequency of spiritual light that

May we have your comments on this book?

We hope that you have enjoyed this book and that it will occupy a special place in your library. It would be helpful to us in meeting your needs and the needs of our readers if you would fill out and mail this postage-free card to us.

Book title: _____

Your comments: _____

_____

_____

_____

How did this book come to your attention? _____

How would you rate this book on a scale of 1 to 5, with 5 being the highest? _____

Topics of interest to you: _____

Would you like to receive a free catalog of our publications? ☐ Yes ☐ No

Name _____ Address _____

City _____ State _____ Zip Code _____ Phone no. _____

(We will not make your name available to other companies.)

E-mail: _____

Thank you for taking the time to give us your feedback.

In the U.S.A., call us toll free at 1-800-245-5445. Outside the U.S.A, call 406-848-9500. E-mail: tslinfo@tsl.org
Summit University Press titles are available from fine bookstores everywhere.

491-AOH 9/00

SUMMIT
UNIVERSITY
PRESS®

*Publisher of fine
spiritual books
since 1975*

BUSINESS REPLY MAIL

FIRST-CLASS MAIL   PERMIT NO. 20   GARDINER MT

POSTAGE WILL BE PAID BY ADDRESSEE

S<small>UMMIT</small> U<small>NIVERSITY</small>  P<small>RESS</small>®

PO Box 5000
Gardiner, MT 59030-9900

stimulates mercy, forgiveness and transmutation.

To "transmute" is to change something into a higher form. This term was used centuries ago by alchemists who attempted, on a physical level, to transmute base metals into gold—and, on a spiritual level, to achieve transformation and ultimately eternal life. That is precisely what the violet flame can do. It is a high-frequency spiritual energy that separates out the "gross" elements of our karma from the gold of our true self and transmutes it so we can achieve our highest potential.

Healers, alchemists and adepts have used this high-frequency spiritual energy to bring about energetic balance and spiritual transformation. Twentieth-century seer Edgar Cayce recognized the healing power of the violet light. Author and three-time near-death survivor Dannion Brinkley has seen and experienced the violet flame in his near-death sojourns.

"The violet flame is the purest place of love. It's what really empowers you," he says. "The violet flame is a light that serves all spiritual heritages, that gives respect and dignity to all things. It gives us a way to connect with each other. . . . The greatness of the violet flame is that it doesn't produce heat; it produces love."[6]

What makes the violet flame such a powerful tool? In our physical world, violet light has the highest frequency in the visible spectrum. As Fritjof Capra explains in *The Tao of Physics,* "violet light has a high frequency and a short wavelength and consists therefore of photons of high energy and high momentum."[7] Of all the spiritual flames, the violet flame is closest in vibratory action to the chemical elements and compounds in our physical universe, and therefore it has the greatest ability to interpenetrate and transform matter at atomic and subatomic levels.

Affirmations and prayers that call forth the violet flame of the Holy Spirit can be used as an adjunct to any spiritual practice. Those who have used the violet flame in their prayers and meditations have found that it helps resolve unhealthy patterns of consciousness, transmutes negative karma, dispels inner pain and brings balance into their lives. It creates an awareness and an attunement with the inner self that enhances creativity and increases sensitivity. It helps keep the doors of our heart open, even after we've gone though a painful experience.

Recently Beth shared with us how she used the first affirmation at the end of this section with surprising results. Beth recognized that the relationship between her and her mother was in need of healing, so she decided to start giving this affirmation. One day as she was driving to her mother's house, she centered in her heart and repeated this affirmation over and over.

"My prayers were answered in a wonderful way," she says. "My mom and I actually sat and chatted for three hours as we never have before. A lot of old baggage was cleared as we both aired our hurt feelings without losing our temper. Even though we may not agree with each other 100 percent, now we can at least respect each other and not let hurt feelings keep us apart."

I've seen thousands of people work successfully with the violet flame. It takes a different amount of time for each person to see results, anywhere from a day to several months. But if you remain constant, you will begin to feel the difference.

I always recommend that those who are new to the violet flame experiment with it. I tell them to give violet-flame prayers and affirmations for at least a month, fifteen minutes a day, and to note the positive changes that start to take place in their life. You can give these affirmations during your daily prayer ritual, while you're in the shower or getting ready for the day, or even as you travel to work, exercise or do your errands.

HEART PERSPECTIVES

• **Clear the heart with prayers, affirmations and visualization.** The following affirmations have helped many people attune with their loving heart and clear blocks within the heart. With regular use, they can create a spiritual climate around the heart that helps us become more open, sensitive and compassionate to ourselves and to the plight of so many who need our love and prayers.

These affirmations invoke the alchemy of the violet flame to clear the painful memories of past experiences. They can also help clear the subconscious, which accepts the judgments of peers and authority figures who have put us down or intimidated us. The violet flame can resolve these patterns of consciousness and free us to be more of our real self.

Many affirmations use the name of God "I AM" to access spiritual power. "I AM" is short for "I AM THAT I AM," the name of God revealed to Moses when he saw the burning bush. "I AM THAT I AM" means simply but profoundly *As above, so below. As God is in heaven, so God is on earth within me. Right where I stand, the power of God is.* Thus every time you say, "I AM . . . ," you are really affirming "God in me is. . . ."

These affirmations for clearing the heart are easy to remember. You can give them aloud every day as part of your spiritual practice and especially when things aren't going well or you feel a heaviness around your heart. Visualize violet-colored flames within your heart softening and then melting away any hardness of heart—transforming anger into compassion, bitterness into sweetness, anxiety into peace. You can recite any affirmation once, three times or as many times as you want until you feel your heart responding to the healing power of love.

AFFIRMATIONS FOR CLEARING THE HEART

I AM a being of violet fire,
I AM the purity God desires!

My heart is a chakra* of violet fire,
My heart is the purity God desires!

Violet fire, thou love divine,
Blaze within this heart of mine!
Thou art mercy forever true,
Keep me always in tune with you.

---

*The heart is one of the seven major energy centers, or chakras, in the body (see pages 161–63 for more on the heart chakra).

PART FOUR

GUARDING
the Heart

*In today's fast-paced world, we are often
bombarded by outer and inner pressures that
can disturb the peaceful and harmonious rhythms of
our heart. Spiritual mastery demands that we guard
our heart against those intruders that would move us
from the center of love. If we are to master the heart,
we must learn to match the rhythm of our living
to the natural rhythm of the heart.*

Keeping Watch in the Heart

The slightest sound matters.
The most momentary rhythm matters.
You can do as you please, yet everything matters.

—*WALLACE STEVENS*

The adept Djwal Kul tells a wonderful story about a town by the sea in Holland where the people were much happier and wiser than the other inhabitants of their land. No one could ever understand why, but Djwal Kul says it was the result of the gentle miller and his wife, who put so much love into their work. The townspeople carried this love home in sacks of flour and then baked it into their bread.

At every meal the regenerative power of love from the miller and his wife radiated around the table and entered the bodies of the townsfolk as they partook of the bread. "Like radioactive power," says Djwal Kul, "the energy of this vibrant love from the miller and his wife was spread throughout the community." He says that just as food prepared by hands charged with divine love can create spiritual happiness, so our actions imbued with love will enhance the beauty of the world community.

Your heart has great healing potential. And there will be times when someone will need a direct infusion of love from your heart. Although we can all be an instrument of healing, we do not become one automatically. In order for our heart to be a reservoir of healing light, ready on a moment's notice to give that infusion of love, we have to open our heart and expand our love. But we also have to guard the heart.

We jeopardize our ability to be an instrument of healing when we cannot hold on to the light that God has given us—when we allow that energy to be drained through outbursts of anger, irritation, pride, intolerance, selfishness, criticism, et cetera. God wants to entrust us with more light and energy, but we have to merit that added increment of power. In other words, the cosmic bank won't lend us more energy than we can prove we will use judiciously.

The unruly intruders who run riot in our heart when we are not on guard also cause us to lose the valuable ground we have gained. "How much more grievous are the consequences of anger than the causes of it," wrote Marcus Aurelius in his *Meditations*. The eighth-century Buddhist monk and sage Shantideva put it this way: "Whatever my virtuous deeds, devotion to Buddhas, generosity, and so on, amassed over a thousand eons, all are destroyed in one moment of fury. There is no sin as harmful as hate, no penance as effective as tolerance.... My mind will not experience peace if it fosters painful thoughts of hatred."[1]

Saint Symeon the New Theologian, a tenth-century Byzantine monk and mystic, said that guarding the heart is the chief task of the spiritual seeker. We must attentively "be on patrol" in our heart, he says. To

> "He that is slow to anger is better than the mighty; and he that ruleth his spirit than he that taketh a city."
>
> —PROVERBS

make his point, Symeon cites Jesus' reply to the scribes and Pharisees who accuse the disciples of transgressing the law because they do not wash their hands before eating bread.

Jesus tries to make them understand that it's not what we do on the outside, like rituals and outer appearances, that makes us holy; it's what takes place within our heart. "Not that which goeth into the mouth defileth a man; but that which cometh out of the mouth," says Jesus. And those things that come out of the mouth "come forth from the heart." In other words, the condition of our heart colors our words and our actions. Jesus goes on to say that from the heart can "proceed evil thoughts" as well as the "things which defile a man," like murders, adulteries, thefts, false witness and blasphemies.

Therefore watching over the heart, says Saint Symeon, is so important that the holy fathers "abandoned all other forms of spiritual labor and concentrated completely on this one task of guarding the heart, convinced that through this practice they would also come to possess every other virtue."[2]

One particularly subtle form of danger that proceeds "from the heart," a danger that can be as corrosive as rage, is the force of irritability. In the Agni Yoga books, the adept El Morya describes the poison resulting from irritability as "imperil."

Imperil is a toxin that can infect, weaken and ultimately destroy. It can make projects fail, relationships fall apart and businesses disintegrate. Imperil can spread like a virus unless we decide to stop the chain reaction, hold the line and meet the force of irritation with absolute harmony. If we tie into the pattern of imperil instead of guarding our heart, we take on that same energy and add our momentum to it. We become a carrier of this infectious disease.

What is the antidote to the poison of irritability? "We place our confidence in the power of patience," says El Morya. "In the intensity of patience a special substance is created which, like a powerful antidote, neutralizes even imperil."[3] Patience is a potent form of love.

In a similar vein, one of my spiritual mentors once said to me, "It's not enough to stand for the truth. It's not enough to stand for the right causes. You must do it with a perfect love and a perfect heart. You must not contain anything of hatred or resentment, because you will instantaneously attract more of that darkness to you. Whatever is inside of you, you will attract." The more intense the opposition to our love, the more we must love.

That's what Tony tried to pass on to his son when he came to him for advice about how to work with his children when they needed disciplining. His son was worried that he wasn't handling it right. Tony has been through a lot since he raised his son. Now Tony meditates on his heart every day as part of his spiritual practice, and he understands how important heart-centeredness is. When his son came to him for advice, he was grateful that he could share what he had learned over the years.

Tony gave his son the honesty and support he needed. He told his son that the way he had raised him was not necessarily the best way. "The only way to raise your children," Tony advised, "is with love." Although that love may at times have to be firm, it always comes from a centered place in the heart, he said. "Never do anything out of anger. If you feel deep anger churning in you, look in the mirror. The person you're angry with is probably yourself."

Tony went on to tell his son that when we deal with children out of love, we have an incredible opportunity to nip potential problems in the bud. "When you're angry," he said, "dig into your reservoir of love. If you still feel there's a need to discuss whatever occurred, do it out of love. In anger, no one hears anything."

Tony is right that the only real way to deal with the forces of anti-love that would try to unseat us is to *radiate more love*. If we send out flood tides of love, then the opposition to that love will not be able to withstand the pressure of the waterfall of light surging through our heart.

HEART PERSPECTIVES

• **Cool off and count to nine.** We all have to deal with circumstances that test our patience and harmony and tempt us to get angry. "The best cure for anger," said Seneca, "is delay." If you are attending a meeting, for instance, and find yourself or someone else getting hot under the collar, try suggesting a fifteen-minute break.

Cool down with a glass of water, get outside for some fresh air and do some deep breathing. Resolve that you will not be moved from your center of harmony by anyone or anything connected with your meeting. Affirm three times out loud with love and determination, *"I shall not be moved from the harmony and love that lives within my heart!"* Having so resolved, consciously turn over to God the matter at hand.

To help control runaway emotions and riptides of negative energy that come up from time to time, you can also use the following prayer as a safety valve. Give it aloud with fervor and know that your Higher Self is in total control of your energies, your meeting and your life.

COUNT TO NINE

Come now by love divine,
Guard thou this soul of mine,
Make now my world all thine,
God's light around me shine.

I count one, it is done.
O feeling world, be still!
Two and three, I AM free,
Peace, it is God's will.

I count four, I do adore
My Presence all divine.
Five and six, O God, affix
My gaze on thee sublime!

I count seven, come, O heaven,
My energies take hold!
Eight and nine, completely thine,
My mental world enfold!

The white-fire light now encircles me,
All riptides are rejected!
With God's own might around me bright
I AM by love protected!

I accept this done right now with full power! I AM this done right now with full power! I AM, I AM, I AM God-life expressing perfection all ways at all times. This which I call forth for myself I call forth for every man, woman and child on this planet!

 # Spiritual Protection

Let us put on the armour of light.   —THE APOSTLE PAUL

Today there is a lot of talk about the mind-body connection and the importance of positive thinking. Researchers are proving that our thoughts and feelings can significantly shape our achievements and health, for better or for worse. A positive attitude can work wonders—and negative thoughts and feelings, our own and another's, can pack a wallop.

Vibrations like anxiety, anger, envy, ridicule, deception, possessiveness and the like are not native to the rhythms of the heart. Like an emotional Mack truck charging straight toward you, these aggressive vibrations can literally floor you. They can cause accidents. They can hit you as a headache or make you feel dense, irritable and out of sorts. They can feel like sudden waves of anxiety or flashes of anger. Sometimes these energies of anti-love can enter your home, disrupt your family life and cause major upheavals.

When you feel this kind of energy surfacing around you or within you, seemingly out of nowhere, you may be tempted to blame yourself or to blame those close to you. Such conditions may be a signal that you have some interior work to do to come back into the center of your heart. But they could also be a warning that you must rise in defense of your right to give and receive love. For at the nexus where love meets love, there is always intense opposition to the manifestation of that love.

For every action there is an equal and opposite reaction. When you determine to embody more love, you can expect that you will face the force of anti-love. Every time you want to move higher on the spiral of love, you will face the opposition to love on that turn of the spiral. As the saying goes, and there is some truth to it, "No good deed goes unpunished." You may find, for example, that those who are jealous of your loving relationship or your new endeavor will try to destroy it.

The forces of the human ego that react to our love with envy, hatred and anger are trying to move us from our centeredness in love. They are trying to get *us* to engage in envy, hatred or anger.

The Flemish mystic Hadewijch of Antwerp wrote, "My distress is great and unknown to men. They are cruel to me, for they wish to dissuade me from all that the forces of Love urge me to. They do not understand it, and I cannot explain it to them. I must then live out what I am; what Love counsels my spirit, in this is my being."[4] The saints and adepts understand that love requires us to stand fast and not back down by lowering the intensity of the flame of love that glows in our heart.

While you are working on a peaceful resolution to any situation, you can guard your heart by establishing a field of protection around it. From the sun center of your being—your heart—you can take command of your inner forces. The human ego may try to pull you off the path of love, but by staying centered in your heart you can remain in control and at peace.

That is what Gautama Buddha learned. According to Buddhist tradition, when Gautama was meditating beneath the Bo tree, intent on gaining enlightenment, all hell broke loose around him to take him off course. First the Evil One, Mara, tried to convince him that it was too hard to keep up his struggle. Then Mara paraded voluptuous goddesses and dancing girls before Gautama. When this didn't work, he assailed the future Buddha with hurricanes, torrential rains, flaming rocks, boiling mud, fierce soldiers, beasts and finally darkness. As a last resort, Mara challenged Gautama's right to be doing what he was doing—his right to gain enlightenment.

> *I bind me today,*
> *God's might to direct me,*
> *God's power to protect me,*
> *God's wisdom for learning,*
> *God's eye for discerning.*
>
> —SAINT PATRICK

Gautama remained unmoved. He tapped the ground, and the earth thundered in response, "I bear you witness!" Gautama's hand gesture has become known as the earth-touching mudra, signifying the unshakableness of the one who declares his right to walk a spiritual path, to bear the flame of love, to become one with God. In order to bear that love and fulfill his life's mission, Gautama had to first defend his right to love.

Whenever we decide to walk the path of the heart, we too have to champion and defend that love. We have to be the warrior of peace who stands fast against the forces of anti-love, from within or without, that try to separate us from those we love. They will try to keep us from maintaining our own personal relationship with God. They will try to erode our sense of self-esteem so that we don't feel worthy of being loved or of loving.

How do we deal with anti-love? First, the adepts tell us to remember that it is not the people who seem to oppose our love that we should focus on, but the energy that is coming through them. It is "anger, my real enemy," says Shantideva, that creates suffering.[5] The first step is to depersonalize the anger, irritation or jealousy being directed at us.

Secondly, as we mentioned in the last section, the adepts say that the only way to deal with anti-love, no matter how intense, is to generate more love. It is the light and fire of the heart that meets the oncoming darkness and consumes it.

Only a heart full of the fire of love can face another's irritation or discord without an automatic reflex of irritation and discord. Only a heart full of love is sensitive enough to realize that the irritation or anger is really a cry for help. Only a mature heart can greet harshness with the affirmation of Shantideva: "May I be the doctor and the medicine and may I be the nurse for all sick beings in the world."[6]

Sometimes guarding the heart means drawing loving boundaries. I have learned this lesson the hard way over the years. Once someone phoned me and all their frustrations came tumbling out in a tirade of anger. After I hung up, I felt as if I had taken into my body and into my heart the pain that was coming to me through that telephone call. I realized that the most loving thing I could have done, for myself and for the person on the other end of the phone, was to politely but firmly draw my boundaries.

When people are angry, we always have a choice. No matter how disturbed they are, we can remain centered in our heart. We can gently explain that we will be happy to talk to them later when they are feeling better, but just now we will have to conclude the conversation.

When people confront us or complain about us, there is usually something for us to learn. In humility, we can listen and see if what they are saying rings true in our heart. There does come a time, however, when the discrimination of your heart tells you that you have to draw the line.

If a situation or a relationship is so full of criticism, discord or abuse that it is toxic, then for the sake of our own spiritual growth we have a right to explain, "I have to move on. There is nothing that my love can do to help you right now. You'll have to find what you need some other way." Or if someone is about to make a serious mistake, you may have to say, "This is unhealthy for you and for me. I can have no part in it. And I recommend you leave it behind also. Let's go forward together in love."

Not only is the heart sensitive to toxic thoughts and feelings, it is also sensitive to the environment —to noise and jagged rhythms as well as stresses at work and at home. In today's world we cannot always avoid these pressures, but we can learn to deal with them.

Saint Germain once gave this practical advice for dealing with these stresses when they come our way: "Often it is a matter of stance. . . . If you slouch, if you are laid-back, wide open, lounging around—the TV set is on, the ads are bombarding. . . , the cat is meowing, the dog is barking, the children are screaming, the phone is ringing—how do you expect, then, to keep your cool? It is a setup, but you have allowed it.

"Now, you can maintain your calm in the midst of these things but not with a laid-back attitude, for any moment the potatoes on the stove will burn and everyone will be in an argument and, if you don't watch out, yourself included.... It's a matter of one, two, three, four, five—a few simple requirements: Do not allow the family to be bombarded from all directions. Do not allow all these things to be taking place at once.

"Strive for communion with the heart. Feed the cat, put out the dog, turn off the TV set, make sure all is safe on the stove, and enjoy that circle of communion with God-determination that each member of your family or household or friends shall have the opportunity, by your loving presence, to express something very important from the heart."[7]

An effective technique to help guard the heart is to meditate on and call forth the protective white light. In his epistles, the apostle Paul advised us to "put on the whole armour of God" and "the armour of light." The saints and mystics of the world's religions have seen the white light in their meditations and prayers. A "pillar of a cloud" by day and "a pillar of fire" by night accompanied the Israelites as they journeyed through the wilderness. And God promised through the prophet Zechariah: "I will be unto her [Jerusalem] a wall of fire around about, and will be the glory in the midst."

The white light can help you stay centered and at peace. It can guard you from negative energies that may be directed at you through someone's anger, condemnation, hatred or jealousy. "Imagine you are light" is the formula of one thirteenth-century Kabbalist. He wrote: "Whatever one implants firmly in the mind becomes the essential thing. So if you pray and offer a blessing to God, or if you wish your intention to be true, imagine you are light. All around you—in every corner and on every side—is light.

> *O God, give me light in my heart... and light in my hearing and light in my sight... and light before me and light behind me.*
>
> —ABU TALIB

"Turn to your right, and you will find shining light; to your left, splendor, a radiant light. Between them, up above, the light of the Presence. Surrounding that, the light of life. Above it all, a crown of light—crowning the aspirations of thought, illumining the paths of imagination, spreading the radiance of vision. This light is unfathomable and endless."[8]

HEART PERSPECTIVES

• **Depersonalize what seems personal.** When faced with a challenging situation, step back and ask your heart what is the real cause of another's anger, irritation or dislike that seems to be directed at you but is really symptomatic of a deeper malaise. Rather than react to the symptom, act from your heart to try and help heal the cause of their upset.

• **Draw boundaries when necessary.** Is there a situation in your life or a toxic relationship that is draining your energy or trying to get you to act in unloving ways? How can you draw loving boundaries in this situation?

• **To enhance your spiritual protection, meditate on the white light.** You can summon the protective white light with the following "Tube of Light" affirmation. The tube of light is a shield of energy that descends from God through your Higher Self in answer

to your call. It's best to give this affirmation each morning before the hustle and bustle of the day begins, preferably giving it three times. If throughout the day you feel de-energized, depleted or vulnerable, withdraw for a few minutes and repeat this affirmation.

As you say these words, see yourself as depicted in the Chart of Your Divine Self on the previous page. Your Higher Self is directly above you. Above your Higher Self is your I AM Presence, the presence of God with you.

See and feel a waterfall of dazzling white light, brighter than the sun shining on new-fallen snow, tumbling down from your I AM Presence to envelop you. See it coalescing to form an impenetrable wall of light.

Inside that scintillating aura of white light, see yourself surrounded with the violet flame of the Holy Spirit, the high-frequency spiritual energy that transforms negativity (your own or another's) into positive and loving energy (see pages 122–28). As you give this prayer aloud, you are affirming that God and the power of God within you are in control of your family, your relationships, your work, your world.

TUBE OF LIGHT

Beloved I AM Presence bright,
Round me seal your tube of light
From ascended master flame
Called forth now in God's own name.
Let it keep my temple* free
From all discord sent to me.

I AM calling forth violet fire
To blaze and transmute all desire,
Keeping on in freedom's name
Till I AM one with the violet flame.

---

*The word *temple* here refers to the many aspects of our being, including our body, mind and emotions. As Paul wrote in his letter to the Corinthians, "Know ye not that ye are the temple of God, and that the Spirit of God dwelleth in you?"

The Power of Softness

What is uttered from the heart alone
Will win the hearts of others to your own. —GOETHE

"The softest, most pliable thing in the world," teaches Lao Tzu in the Tao Te Ching, "runs roughshod over the firmest thing in the world." Lao Tzu was talking about the tremendous power of water to attack the hardest of rocks. He was talking about the ultimate power of softness. Expanding the analogy, he says, "One who is good in battle doesn't get angry; one who is good at defeating the enemy doesn't engage him."

A child's caress, a simple smile or a kind and understanding word can do more to create positive change than any amount of force. In our book *Your Seven Energy Centers,* we talk about softness as a receptive mode where unnatural, forceful human actions and reactions give way to the natural movement of the heart. Softness is a nurturing, giving attitude that does not take offense. Softness is the opposite of brittleness, rigidity or resistance. Brittle things can break, but softness is flexible and can bend. As a wise commentator once said,

"Blessed are the flexible, for they shall not be bent out of shape."

We explained that this is the principle behind martial arts like T'ai Chi Ch'uan. These arts are based on cultivating inner strength and developing softness that will triumph over the use of external, muscular force. The body appears to be soft and gentle externally but has a great concentration of internal power.

The twentieth-century T'ai Chi Ch'uan master Cheng Man-ch'ing taught that true mastery and energy come from softness not hardness, flexibility not force. Wolfe Lowenthal, who published the master's teaching, says he taught that gentleness, sensitivity and compassion are the secret to mastering the martial arts.

"A person compensates for internal weakness by becoming aggressive and defensive," he said, but "hard energy blocks the flow of *ch'i* [our energy or life-force]; it is a disjointed expression of a fraction of our potential strength." Soft energy, on the other hand, is consistent with *ch'i* and does not block its flow. For example, the power of an arrow comes from the elasticity, softness and aliveness of the bow and string, taught the master. "It is a paradox," he said, "that real softness can only come from strength."[9]

Renowned trial lawyer Gerry Spence gives an example of this in his book *How to Argue and Win Every Time* in a section on winning *without* arguing. He says he learned this precept from his wife after they first returned from their honeymoon. He wanted to show his new wife that he was in charge and was setting his own ground rules. So he purposely went out for a cup of coffee with a friend after work and did not come home for dinner on time. He was especially sensitive to this because this had been a source of contention in a previous relationship.

When he finally arrived home, over an hour late, his new wife greeted him with a big kiss and a smile. Without complaint, she said she had eaten already but had kept his dinner warm in the oven. He was shocked that she was not angry with him.

He tried the same thing again the next night, thinking maybe this was all an act. Again, his wife treated him in the same loving way, even though he never apologized for being late. When he asked her if she wasn't even a little mad, she told him that she was certain he had been busy at the office and that full-grown men didn't need someone telling them when to come home to supper.

"She won our first argument without arguing," says Spence, "and I have never since intentionally been late for supper in all of the years we've been married.... Trust begets trust, and I became trustworthy. I learned again that night what I had learned so many times before and forgotten as often—that demonstrations of love, whether in the kitchen, the bedroom, or the courtroom, are the most powerful of all arguments."[10]

> To those who are good to me I am good; and to those who are not good to me, I am also good; and thus all get to be good.
>
> —TAO TE CHING

The power of softness and openness, as opposed to harshness and being close-minded, is the driving force behind the principle of meaningful dialogue. The late physicist David Bohm, a founder of MIT's dialogue project, says that the word *dialogue* derives from *dia* (through) and *logos* (the word). Thus, *dialogue* describes a process of meaning flowing through and around the participants.

In a paper on dialogue, David Bohm, Donald Factor and Peter Garrett explain that a dialogue is neither a debate (which implies that one opinion will prevail over another) nor a discussion—a word that shares a root meaning with *percussion* and *concussion,* which have to do with breaking things up. In a real dialogue, we suspend our assumptions and freely exchange ideas and information. By so doing, we reach a place that none of us could have reached on our own.

Joan, a meeting facilitator, reminds the people in the groups she helps that sometimes we have to give up our own agendas to reach the greater truth. "Successful meetings happen when we strike a balance between advocacy and inquiry—when we not only explain our own viewpoint but when we also inquire. Instead of always promoting our own cause, we can ask questions to try and understand another's point of view. That's when we make the most headway."

HEART PERSPECTIVES

• **Inquire more often.** The next time you are in a discussion or meeting, be open to arriving at a new understanding that you may not have thought of before. Try to spend as much time asking questions and exploring options as you do advocating your position and see what happens.

• **Try a little softness.** Can you remember an incident when your use of force rather than softness blocked progress? Can you think of a time when your use of softness rather than hardness helped you get the results you wanted without strain or stress? Is there a situation in your life right now where you can apply greater softness?

PART FIVE

ENTERING
the Heart

The heart is the place of great encounters.
It is the place where we meet our Real Self and
where we meet God. Whenever this encounter takes
place, there is an alchemical transformation and
we are never again the same.

 # The Secret Chamber

The supreme heaven shines in the lotus of the heart.

—*KAIVALYA UPANISHAD*

From Christian contemplatives to Buddhist meditation masters, the world's mystics have discovered the magic of communion with the Divine in their heart. They describe the heart as the nexus between this world and the spiritual world. There, halfway between heaven and earth, they say, we can seek and find our essential reality.

Thus the heart is more than a physical organ; it is the seat of our higher consciousness and the springboard for self-transformation. In Eastern tradition, the heart is the fulcrum of the body's energy system. It is one of seven major energy centers, known as chakras. Each chakra is symbolically depicted as a lotus that has a different number of petals.

These centers function at subtle levels, invisible to the physical eye, yet they affect every aspect of our life. They are like receiving- and sending-stations that process and step down the spiritual energy that flows to us moment by moment, nourishing body, mind and soul.

As we explain in greater detail in *Your Seven Energy Centers,* the heart is the most important energy center in the body. Just as oxygenated blood from our lungs is pumped by the heart to the rest of the body, so the energy we receive from Spirit passes through our heart center before it moves on to nourish the other chakras and systems of our body.

As energy passes through our heart chakra, it takes on its imprint—the unique vibration and quality of our heart. That imprint, for better or worse, affects everything we say and do. As the author of Proverbs said, "As [a man] thinketh in his heart, so is he." That is why it is so important to heal and clear the heart with techniques like those we discussed in Part Three on "Healing the Heart."

Each of our spiritual centers, or chakras, provides a different way for us to perceive and receive God. Through the heart chakra we can choose to experience God as love, compassion, charity, comfort, softness, sensitivity, discernment and appreciation. Or we can choose to misuse the creative energy that flows through our heart and express it as hatred, dislike, anger, selfishness, irritation and negligence.

The mystics describe the heart as a place of refuge where we can retreat to talk to God. "The heart is nothing but the Sea of Light," wrote Rumi, "the place of the vision of God." Hindu and Buddhist writings tell us that the heart is the abiding place of "the Lord of All."

The mystics also reveal that within our heart there is an antechamber, so to speak. This is your inner temple, tabernacle, cathedral—your private meditation room. In Hinduism this inner sanctuary is known as the eighth chakra, called *Ananda-Kanda* ("root of bliss"). It is also called the secret, or hidden, chamber of the heart. Jesus described the secret chamber when he said, "When thou prayest, enter into thy closet, and when thou hast shut thy door, pray to thy Father which is in secret."

The secret chamber of the heart is a doorway into cosmic dimensions. "The little space within the heart is as great as this vast universe," the ancient Chandogya Upanishad says. "The heavens and the earth are there, and the sun and the moon and the stars; fire and lightning and winds are there; and all that now is and all that is not." One Sanskrit text exhorts us to enter into meditation by visualizing a beautiful island in our heart, where golden sands are sprinkled with jewels, and fragrant blossoming trees line the shores. Under a beautiful arbor is a temple of rubies, where we commune with our teacher in deep meditation.

As we move through our heart chakra in meditation, there is, as it were, a door at the rear that leads to the secret chamber. There, seated upon a throne, is our inner teacher, our Higher Self. This beloved friend who provides divine guidance and spiritual connection is known in various spiritual traditions by different names.

> *Concealed in the heart of all beings is the Atman, the Spirit, the Self; smaller than the smallest atom, greater than the vast spaces.*
>
> —KATHA UPANISHAD

Hindu tradition describes the indwelling spirit who lives in the heart as "the inmost Self, no bigger than a thumb," also known as the Atman. Christian mystics refer to the inner man of the heart or the Inner Light. Jesus discovered the Higher Self to be "the Christ" and Gautama discovered it to be "the Buddha." Thus that Higher Self is sometimes called the Inner Christ (or Christ Self) or the Inner Buddha.

The special acoustics of the secret chamber of the heart allow us to hear the "still small voice" of

God and our Higher Self and to receive the divine direction and understanding we so desperately need. So often we think we're too busy to stop and listen. Yet the secret chamber isn't very far away. It doesn't have to take long to slip in and have a quick conference call with your inner teacher.

HEART PERSPECTIVES

• **Consult frequently with your inner teacher.** Your Higher Self knows all. It can teach you, give you unerring direction and warn you of danger if you will take the time to tune in to that voice. Once you acknowledge this masterful presence within, you can retreat to your secret chamber at key points in your day and commune with that one. You can say: *"O Beloved One, I am so grateful for your guidance, illumination and love. Teach me. Direct the course of my life and show me the next steps I must take."*

You can go into your heart, make the connection with your Higher Self, and ask specific questions you need answers to, such as what action to take next or how to resolve a situation that has come up. The next step is one of the most important: *listen.* The answer may not come immediately, but at the right time it will come.

❤ A Spark of the Divine

The body itself is a screen to shield and partially reveal
the light that's blazing inside your presence.   —RUMI

The mystics have also revealed that blazing
within the secret chamber of the heart is
a "divine spark"—a sacred flame that God has
endowed us with, a spark of fire from God's own
heart. In essence, the divine spark is a portion of
God right inside of you. It is pure Spirit. It is your
point of contact with your Source. We may believe
we are walking the earth as human beings, but we
are in fact divine beings with a divine connection.

Mystics the world around believe that a part
of God resides within each of us. "Know ye not
that . . . the Spirit of God dwelleth in you?" wrote
the apostle Paul. In Hindu tradition, the Katha
Upanishad speaks of the "light of the Spirit" that
is concealed in the "secret high place of the heart"
of all beings. The Jewish mystics refer to a divine
spark within, the *neshamah,* which serves as a
bridge to the divine world.

Those who have contacted this divine spark
describe it as a sacred fire as well as a seed of the

Divine. Saint Catherine of Siena said in one of her prayers: "In your nature, eternal Godhead, I shall come to know my nature. And what is my nature . . . ? It is fire, because you are nothing but a fire of love. . . . You who are fire share the fire with [the soul]."[1]

The Christian theologian and mystic Meister Eckhart said, "God's seed is within us." There is a part of us, says Eckhart, that "remains eternally in the Spirit and is divine. . . . Here God glows and flames without ceasing." Similarly Buddhists speak of the divine spark as the "germ

> *The soul is kissed by God in its innermost regions.*
> —HILDEGARD OF BINGEN

of Buddhahood" that exists in every living being.

Buddhist texts explain that "all that lives is endowed with the Essence of the Buddha"—the Buddha nature. Buddhist writings and works of art often symbolize the heart as a lotus, which when nurtured unfolds to reveal that Buddha nature. Within every one of us, that lotus of the heart is destined to blossom and unfold our full spiritual potential.

In some traditions, this spark is called a "threefold" flame because it engenders the primary attributes of Spirit—power, wisdom and love, corresponding to the Trinity. We draw upon this inner flame every time we act from the loving, spiritual part of ourselves. It is the fire, the verve, the creative spark that imbues our finest thoughts and feelings, words and deeds. This flame is spiritual power—the power to change our own lives and ultimately to change the world.

Your divine spark is the same universal light that has burned in the hearts of the saints, adepts and ascended masters* of East and West. The only difference between their flame and our flame is its size and intensity. The more intense the flame, the greater the endowment of light. The greater the light, the more power we have to become living transformers of love.

Like the great revolutionaries of the Spirit, we can increase the size and intensity of our spiritual flame and our empowerment of love. The mystics have given us several formulas to expand that light. Their formulas involve the exercise of heart, head and hand, because we don't expand the flame only

*The ascended masters are those from all the world's spiritual traditions who have fulfilled their reason for being, graduated from earth's schoolroom and reunited with God.

through meditation and prayer. We also expand it through the practical application of our heart—the actions we take every day to meet another's need.

In the first four sections of this book, we discussed some of the practical ways to open, heal and empower the heart. In the next section, we will explore how to stoke the fires of the heart through prayer and meditation as we enter our interior castle, our sacred lotus, our secret chamber of the heart.

 # Heart-Centered Prayer

Our prayers should be burning words coming forth from the furnace of a heart filled with love. —*MOTHER TERESA*

The revolutionaries of the Spirit have discovered how to harness the fires of the heart. Through the white-hot heat of meditation and prayer, we too can release the imprisoned lightning of our heart.

Our meditations in the secret chamber are very private experiences. They start with removing our attention from what's happening around us and going within—"all the gates closed, the mind confined in the heart," as the Bhagavad Gita says. Christian tradition calls it recollection, withdrawing the mind from external affairs and placing our attention on the presence of God within.

When we go within by devotion and love, we contact the inner flame and commune with the energy that is God. "The little spirit spark of our personal identity is the key that connects us with the Universal," Mark Prophet once said. "[God's] Spirit is the fabric of our world. His energy, his pattern is the only saving grace. We ourselves have to reidentify, reintegrate, repolarize ourselves with that light—and it's got to be done consciously."

Through prayer and meditation we turn our attention back to the Inner Light, which is the real source of our being. We become drenched with light—renewed, refreshed and replenished—so we can give more of the light to those who need it. We build up our reservoir of love. As we commune with our Higher Self, who sits on the throne in our heart, we can also access the wisdom of the heart to find solutions to knotty problems.

The mystics advise us to combine our meditations with spoken prayer that comes from a heart on fire with love. For instance, the Zohar instructs,

"Whatever a man thinks or whatever he meditates in his heart cannot be realized in fact until he enunciates it with his lips." The spoken word activates the fruit of our meditation upon the Divine and coalesces it in the physical.

Every spiritual tradition has its own beautiful methods for entering the heart through prayer and meditation—from the quiet recitation of sacred words to the dynamic repetition of mantras to the inspired singing of devotional songs, like bhajans. The following section begins with a short meditation you can use daily to enter your heart. It is followed by heart-centered meditations and prayers from the world's spiritual traditions. (The meditations are in roman type and the prayers are in italic.)

Each prayer can be said aloud once or repeated many times, like a mantra, as you enter into deeper and deeper communion with your heart. You are welcome to use any or all of these offerings to enhance your own spiritual practice. May they help you create a richer experience with the divine presence who is waiting for you within the inner recesses of your heart.

Prayers and Meditations for Entering the Heart

A burning heart is what I want; consort with burning!
Kindle in thy heart the flame of love.   —RUMI

> Let the words of my mouth
> And the meditation of my heart
> Be acceptable in thy sight,
> O Lord, my strength and my redeemer.
>
> Create in me a clean heart, O God,
> And renew a right spirit within me.
>
> —Psalms

Meditation for Entering the Secret Chamber

Enter your sacred space.

You are about to begin the most important experience of every day of your life. It is a sacred ritual you can do once, or more than once, a day.

First find a quiet place where you will be undisturbed. Many people find that dedicating a room or part of a room for spiritual rituals and creating their own personal altar helps them make the sacred connection more easily.[2]

Be seated in a comfortable chair with your legs uncrossed and your feet flat on the floor or sit in a lotus posture. Keep your spine erect in honor of the Spirit within you. These positions are the most conducive to the flow of energy through your spiritual centers. You can also separate your hands, cup them and place them on your lap in a receptive mode. Cupping your hands symbolizes that you are offering yourself as a chalice for God: *"Pour thyself into me, O living Spirit."*

Center in your heart.

Once you are seated, close your eyes, take some deep breaths and withdraw your attention from all outer circumstances and cares of this world. Each time you exhale, consciously release the tensions of the day. Let go of the worries, concerns and preoccupations. Withdraw your attention from problems at home and at work, from physical and emotional burdens. Set them all aside for the moment.

Now center all of your energy and attention on your heart chakra in the center of your chest. See in your mind's eye the intensity of the sun at noonday. Transfer the picture of that fiery sphere of light to the center of your chest cavity. You are aware of nothing else but this great sphere of light.

Take another deep breath. As you exhale, visualize yourself gently descending into the sphere of light, energy and consciousness that is your radiant heart chakra. You are entering it entirely, moving farther away from the limiting dimensions of time and space into a timeless, spaceless dimension.

Enter the secret chamber.

As you travel deeper and deeper into the inner recesses of your being, visualize yourself entering the secret chamber of the heart chakra. Visualize yourself walking into this chamber as you would enter a mighty cathedral, a private chapel, a beautiful synagogue, mosque, or Buddhist or Hindu temple.

As you continue your meditation on the secret chamber of the heart, begin to feel the divine stillness of perfect love. This is an inner experience, as though you were alone in the cosmos with your Creator. You are inside of your God; your God is inside of you.

Visualize and feel your divine spark.

As you take your place within the secret chamber, direct your attention to the sacred flame, the divine spark, that burns upon the central altar. The altar of your heart is the place you go for "alteration" —for transformation, for alchemy. We come to this altar to leave behind an outworn portion of our-selves—the "old man," as Paul called it, which is our old habits and patterns—and to garner a greater por-tion of the light of our Higher Self, the "new man." (As you give your prayers, you can visualize yourself shedding the layers of your aura that are ready to be discarded. See them fall to the ground and let them be consumed by the flame.)

Fold your hands at the center of your chest, at the point of your heart chakra. Feel the beating of your heart and see, with your inner eye, the flame that is your divine spark pulsating on that altar within the secret chamber of your heart. You can picture this flame as having three parts, representing the three primary divine attributes (see page 168). On your left is the blue flame, representing divine power. In the middle is the yellow flame, embodying divine wisdom. On your right is the pink flame, which radiates divine love.

Greet your inner teacher.

Here in the secret chamber, before your personal altar, you approach your inner teacher and mentor, your Higher Self. As you stand before your altar, bow before the sacred flame and then before your inner guide. Each time you do so, it is your opportu-nity to offer a heartfelt prayer, such as:

Almighty God, I bow before the flame you have placed in my heart, which is a portion of yourself. My beloved Inner Christ, Inner Buddha, Inner Light, show me this day what you would have me do with the power, wisdom and love of this divine spark so that I may be your heart, your head and your hand in action—my heart, thy heart beating as one.

To increase the intensity of the fire that burns within, take a moment to send an intense arc of love and gratitude from your heart to God and to feel the return current of that love.

Express the inner fire of your devotion and gratitude.

Our prayers, affirmations and mantras are a spoken meditation of our heart. They are a celebration of our spirit. As you say every word, feel the spiritual resonance of that word inside your heart.

The mystics advise us to guard against the rote performance of rituals and good works. What enhances our spirituality is the intention, the motive and the devotion we pour into our rituals, our prayers and our works. The quality of heart we infuse into everything we say and do is what creates the alchemy of change.

Creatively visualize while you pray.

Before you begin your spiritual practice, you can consecrate your prayers to a specific outcome, such as the resolution of a challenging situation at work, at home or on the world scene. Visualizations are like a magnet that attracts the creative energies of Spirit to fill in the blueprint you hold in mind.

Use your imagination to see, as if on a movie screen, the desired outcome of your prayers, the resolution of the situations you are praying for. As you recite your prayers, affirmations or mantras, see the actions described by each word taking place right before your eyes.

While you hold the pictures of these outcomes in mind, stay open to the new and novel. God is extremely creative. Our prayers aren't always answered in the way we expect, but they are always answered in the way we need most.

Meditations on the Flame in the Heart

As you give aloud the prayer "I AM the Light of the Heart," you can visualize thousands of sunbeams going forth from your heart. See intense fiery-pink laser beams penetrate and dissolve any darkness, despair or depression within yourself, within loved ones or within any who need the light from your heart. See these rays of loving-kindness going forth to break down all barriers to the success of your relationships, your family, your spiritual growth, your career, your community and your nation.

I AM the Light of the Heart

I AM the light of the heart
Shining in the darkness of being
And changing all into the golden treasury
Of the mind of Christ.

I AM projecting my love
Out into the world
To erase all errors
And to break down all barriers.

I AM the power of infinite love,
Amplifying itself
Until it is victorious,
World without end!

I AM a Son / a Daughter of God

*I AM a Son/a Daughter of God. This day
I AM charging the substance within my heart
that is mine to command with the flame of love
from the hand of Almighty God.*

*I send it forth from my being everywhere
in all directions to perform the perfect work of
God and to return to me with all the divine love
which I AM sending forth.*

Holy Christ Flame within Me

Holy Christ Self above me,
Thou balance of my soul,
Let thy blessed radiance
Descend and make me whole.*

  *Thy flame within me ever blazes,
  Thy peace about me ever raises,
  Thy love protects and holds me,
  Thy dazzling light enfolds me.
  I AM thy threefold radiance,
  I AM thy living presence
  Expanding, expanding, expanding now.*

(cont.)

---

*The "Holy Christ Self" is another name for your Higher Self.
The "Holy Christ flame" is your divine spark, the threefold
flame that abides within the secret chamber of your heart.

Holy Christ flame within me,
Come, expand thy triune light;
Flood my being with the essence
Of the pink, blue, gold and white.

Thy flame within me ever blazes,
Thy peace about me ever raises,
Thy love protects and holds me,
Thy dazzling light enfolds me.
I AM thy threefold radiance,
I AM thy living presence
Expanding, expanding, expanding now.

Holy lifeline to my Presence,
Friend and brother ever dear,
Let me keep thy holy vigil,
Be thyself in action here.

Thy flame within me ever blazes,
Thy peace about me ever raises,
Thy love protects and holds me,
Thy dazzling light enfolds me.
I AM thy threefold radiance,
I AM thy living presence
Expanding, expanding, expanding now.

Meditation in the Island of the Heart

"To enter into the garden of the heart is to enter a chamber that exists in the mind of God which can come into being as the kingdom of God within you through meditation and through visualization. . . .

"The Eastern devotee sees the earth transformed into jewellike crystals. Emeralds, diamonds, rubies compose the island in the midst of the nectar sea; and the essence of the Spirit Most Holy is the fragrance from flowering trees. You should also use your imagination to create this royal scene...

"It is well to be specific. Therefore, draw a specific outline in your mind of this bejeweled island suspended in a glistening sea. Then see yourself walking from the shores of the sea through the tropical trees and vegetation to the center and highest promontory of the island.

"Tropical birds and flowers of delicate and brilliant colors make the scene more vivid. And by and by you hear the songs of the birds as they sing the song celestial and key the soul to the frequencies of that plane where the ascending triangle of Mater [matter] meets the descending triangle of Spirit.

"When you come to the center of your island in the sun, visualize specifically the platform and the throne that are consecrated for the image and the sacred presence of the master. You may wish to examine historical works showing the most beautiful thrones that have been built for the kings and queens of this world. Select a design that is richly carved, gold leafed, and inlaid with precious and semiprecious stones, and visualize upon it a velvet cushion....

"As you contemplate the blue-skyey dome and this place prepared to receive the Lord, give the following invocation for the integration of your soul with the consciousness of the Christ and its perfect outpicturing in the hidden chamber of the heart."

> *O Lord my God,*
> *Come and talk and walk with me*
> *In this my paradise garden,*
> *My island in the sea!*
>
> *Come, O Lord, in the cool of the day.*
> *Come! For I have prepared the way,*
> *And my offering is the sacrifice of the lesser self*
> *Upon the altar of the heart.*
>
> *I come before thy presence, Lord.*
> *I see thee in thy essence, Lord.*
> *I am thy omnipresence, Lord.*

Teach me how to be thyself,
How to walk the earth
As heart and head and hand
Responding to thy will at thy command.

O Infinite One,
Thou God of all above, below,
It is thyself that I would know.
Come unto me, come into me,
O God of love!
Let me dwell with thee, in thee.[3]

—Djwal Kul

Meditations in the Lotus of the Heart

"The ancient yogis believed that there was an actual center of spiritual consciousness, called 'the lotus of the heart,' situated between the abdomen and the thorax, which could be revealed in deep meditation. They claimed that it had the form of a lotus and that it shone with an inner light. It was said to be 'beyond sorrow,' since those who saw it were filled with an extraordinary sense of peace and joy. . . .

"If the body is thought of as a busy and noisy city, then we can imagine that, in the middle of this city, there is a little shrine, and that, within this shrine, the Atman, our real nature, is present. No matter what is going on in the streets outside, we can always enter that shrine and worship. It is always open."[4]

—Swami Prabhavananda and Christopher Isherwood

"The supreme heaven shines in the lotus of the heart. Those who struggle and aspire may enter there. Retire into solitude. Seat yourself on a clean spot in an erect posture, with the head and neck in a straight line. Control all sense-organs. Bow down in devotion to your teacher. Then enter the lotus of the heart and meditate there on the presence of Brahman*—the pure, the infinite, the blissful."[5]

—Kaivalya Upanishad

In Eastern tradition, the secret chamber of the heart is described as an eight-petaled lotus, or chakra, called **Ananda-Kanda** *("root of bliss"). Within this sanctuary of the heart abides your divine spark, one with Spirit.*

*Brahman is the Ultimate Reality, the Absolute

"Within the city of Brahman, which is the body, there is the heart, and within the heart there is a little house. This house has the shape of a lotus, and within it dwells that which is to be sought after, inquired about, and realized. . . .

"The lotus of the heart, where Brahman resides in all his glory—that, and not the body, is the true city of Brahman. Brahman, dwelling therein, is untouched by any deed, ageless, deathless, free from grief, free from hunger and from thirst. His desires are right desires, and his desires are fulfilled."[6] —Chandogya Upanishad

Lead Us from the Unreal to the Real

There is a light that shines
Beyond all things on earth, beyond us all,
Beyond the heavens, beyond the highest,
    the very highest heavens.
This is the light that shines in our heart!

O Thou that art manifest, be Thou manifest to us:
From the unreal, lead us to the Real;
From darkness lead us to Light;
From death lead us to immortality.   —the Upanishads

Om Mani Padme Hum
(Pronounced Om Mah-nee Pud-may Hoom)
Hail to the jewel in the lotus!*

*See page 15.

Meditation on the Inner Palace

"Consider what St. Augustine says, that he sought [God] in many places but found Him ultimately within himself. Do you think it matters little for a soul with a wandering mind to understand this truth and see that there is no need to go to heaven in order to speak with one's Eternal Father or find delight in Him? Nor is there any need to shout. However softly we speak, He is near enough to hear us. . . .

"Let us imagine that within us is an extremely rich palace, built entirely of gold and precious stones; in sum, built for a lord such as this. Imagine, too, as is indeed so, that you have a part to play in order for the palace to be so beautiful; for there is no edifice as beautiful as is a soul pure and full of virtues. The greater the virtues the more resplendent the jewels. Imagine, also, that in this palace dwells this mighty King who has been gracious enough to become your Father; and that He is seated upon an extremely valuable throne, which is your heart.

. . . All of this imagining is necessary that we may truly understand that within us lies something incomparably more precious than what we see outside ourselves. . . . I consider it impossible for us to pay so much attention to worldly things if we take the care to remember we have a Guest such as this within us, for we then see how lowly these things are next to what we possess within ourselves....

"...What a marvelous thing, that He who would fill a thousand worlds and many more with His grandeur would enclose Himself in something so small! In fact, since He is Lord He is free to do what He wants, and since He loves us He adapts Himself to our size."[7]

—Teresa of Avila

May I See You Today

Dearest Lord, may I see you today and every day in the person of your sick, and, whilst nursing them, minister unto you.

Though you hide yourself behind the unattractive disguise of the irritable, the exacting, the unreasonable, may I still recognize you, and say:

'Jesus, my patient, how sweet it is to serve you.'...

Lord, increase my faith, bless my efforts and work, now and for evermore. Amen.[8]

—Mother Teresa

Light, Give Us Light

O eternal Trinity, my sweet love!
You, light, give us light.
You, wisdom, give us wisdom.
You, supreme strength, strengthen us.

Today, eternal God,
*   let our cloud be dissipated*
*   so that we may perfectly know and*
*   follow your Truth in truth,*
*   with a free and simple heart.*

O fire ever blazing!
The soul who comes to know herself in you
*   finds your greatness wherever she turns,*
*   even in the tiniest things,*
*   in people and in all created things,*
*   for in all of them she sees your power*
*   and wisdom and mercy.*

You, light, make the heart simple,
*   not two-faced.*
You make it big, not stingy—
*   so big that it has room*
*   in its loving charity for everyone.*
Do not be slow, most kind Father,
*   to turn the eye of your mercy*
*   on the world.*[9]

—Catherine of Siena

I Am Your Opus

God says:
Ever
you are
before my eyes.

God, I am your opus.
Before the beginning of time,
already then,
I was in your mind. . . .

Through God I have living spirit.
Through God I have life and movement.
Through God I learn, I find my path.

If I call in truth, this God and
Lord directs my steps;
setting my feet to the rhythm of
his precepts.
I run like a deer that seeks its spring.
I have my home on high.[10]

—Hildegard of Bingen

Grant Us to Love

O Lord, grant us to love Thee; grant that
we may love those that love Thee; grant that we
may do the deeds that win Thy love. Make the
love of Thee to be dearer to us than ourselves,
than our families, than wealth, and even than
cool water.[11]   —Muhammad

May I Become an Inexhaustible Treasure

May I be the doctor and the medicine
And may I be the nurse
For all sick beings in the world
Until everyone is healed....

May I become an inexhaustible treasure
For those who are poor and destitute;
May I turn into all things they could need
And may these be placed close beside them....

And when anyone encounters me
May it never be meaningless for him....
May all who say bad things to me
Or cause me any other harm,
And those who mock and insult me,
Have the fortune to fully awaken.[12]
                                              —Shantideva

May All Be Blessed with Peace

May creatures all abound in weal and peace;
May all be blessed with peace always;
All creatures weak or strong,
All creatures great and small,
Creatures unseen or seen,
Dwelling afar or near,
Born or awaiting birth,
*   —May all be blessed with peace!*[13]

—the Sutta-Nipata

Gate Gate Paragate Parasamgate Bodhi Svaha*
(Pronounced Gah-tay Gah-tay Para-gah-tay
Para-sahm-gah-tay Boh-dee Svah-hah)

Gone, gone, gone beyond, gone wholly beyond—
Enlightenment, hail! (or Awakening fulfilled!)

---

*This is the last line of the popular Heart Sutra, given daily by
many Buddhists. This mantra is said to allay all suffering.

God dwells in the hearts of all beings,
beloved, your God dwells in your heart
and his power of wonder moves all things...
whirling them onwards on the stream of time....

I have given you words of vision and wisdom
more secret than hidden mysteries.
Ponder them in the silence of your heart,
and then, in freedom, do your will.

—THE BHAGAVAD GITA

Notes

Part 1   OPENING THE HEART

1. Malcolm Muggeridge, *Something Beautiful for God* (Garden City, N.Y.: Doubleday & Company, Image Books, 1977), pp. 44, 109.
2. Coleman Barks et al., trans., *The Essential Rumi* (HarperSanFrancisco, 1995), p. 188. The quotes of Rumi cited on pages 7, 66 and 166 are from *The Essential Rumi,* pp. 200, 8, 172.
3. See Jack Kornfield and Christina Feldman, *Soul Food: Stories to Nourish the Spirit and the Heart* (HarperSanFrancisco, 1996), p. 141.
4. Wayne Muller, *Legacy of the Heart: The Spiritual Advantages of a Painful Childhood* (New York: Simon & Schuster, Fireside, 1993), p. 176.
5. Barks et al. *The Essential Rumi,* p. 166.
6. Ibid., p. 109.
7. M. Scott Peck, *The Road Less Traveled: A New Psychology of Love, Traditional Values and Spiritual Growth* (New York: Simon & Schuster, Touchstone, 1978), pp. 81, 116–17.
8. Lorraine E. Hale, *Hale House: Alive with Love* (Hale House, 1991), p. 8.
9. "Slain Journalists Honored by Colleagues, Diplomats," *CNN.com,* 25 May 2000. http://www.cnn.com/2000/WORLD/africa/05/25/slain.journalists.02/ (6 June 2000).

10. Lesia Stockall Cartelli with Barbara Bartocci, "The Fire Within," *Woman's Day,* 16 September 1997, p. 25.

11. Shelley Donald Coolidge, "'Corporate Decency' Prevails at Malden Mills," *Christian Science Monitor,* 28 March 1996.

Part 2   EMPOWERING THE HEART

1. Erika J. Chopich and Margaret Paul, *Healing Your Aloneness: Finding Love and Wholeness through Your Inner Child* (HarperSanFrancisco, 1990), p. 41.

2. Melody Beattie, *Codependent No More: How to Stop Controlling Others and Start Caring for Yourself* (Center City, Minn.: Hazelden, 1992), p. 36.

3. Ibid., p. 37.

4. John Gray, foreword to *Handbook for the Heart: Original Writings on Love,* ed. Richard Carlson and Benjamin Shield (Boston: Little, Brown and Company, 1996), p. *x.*

5. Aung San Suu Kyi with Alan Clements, *The Voice of Hope* (New York: Seven Stories Press, 1997), p. 278.

6. See Elizabeth Clare Prophet with Patricia R. Spadaro and Murray L. Steinman, "The Origin of Evil," in *Kabbalah: Key to Your Inner Power* (Corwin Springs, Mont.: Summit University Press, 1997) pp. 142–45.

7. Harville Hendrix, "The Mirror of Love," in *Handbook for the Heart,* ed. Carlson and Shield, p. 93.

8. Jack Kornfield, "The Wellspring of the Heart," in

Handbook for the Heart, ed. Carlson and Shield, pp. 44–45.

9. Barks et al. *The Essential Rumi,* pp. 190–91.
10. "Eddi Bocelli's Story." http://www.geocities.com/ Vienna/Choir/6642/eddi.html (23 June 2000).
11. David McArthur and Bruce McArthur, *The Intelligent Heart: Transform Your Life with the Laws of Love* (Virginia Beach, Va.: A.R.E. Press, 1997), pp. 40–42. See also Doc Childre and Howard Martin with Donna Beech, *The HeartMath Solution* (HarperSanFrancisco, 1999).
12. Thomas Petzinger Jr., "Talking about Tomorrow: Saul Bellow," *Wall Street Journal Interactive Edition, 2000.* http://interactive.wsj.com/millennium/articles/flash-SB944523384413082346.htm (24 July 2000).

Part 3   HEALING THE HEART

1. Angela Pirisi, "Forgive to Live," *Psychology Today,* July/August 2000, p. 26.
2. Hendrix, "The Mirror of Love," pp. 93–94, 97–98.
3. Just as a ray of sunlight passing through a prism is refracted into the seven colors of the rainbow, so the spiritual light we call forth in our spoken prayer manifests as seven rays, or flames. The violet flame is the color and frequency of spiritual light that stimulates mercy, forgiveness and transmutation. The pink flame is the flame of divine love. (See also pages 122–28.)
4. Tom Gliatto, "The Mourning After," *People,* 30 March 1997.

5. Norman Lebrecht, *Mahler Remembered* (New York: W.W. Norton & Company, 1988), p. 148.
6. Dannion Brinkley, quoted in Elizabeth Clare Prophet with Patricia R. Spadaro and Murray L. Steinman, *Saint Germain's Prophecy for the New Millennium* (Corwin Springs, Mont.: Summit University Press, 1999), pp. 305, 306.
7. Fritjof Capra, *The Tao of Physics,* 2d ed. (New York: Bantam Books, 1984), p. 141.

Part 4   GUARDING THE HEART

1. Robert A. F. Thurman, *Essential Tibetan Buddhism* (HarperSanFrancisco, 1996), p. 142; Acharya Shantideva, *A Guide to the Bodhisattva's Way of Life,* trans. Stephen Batchelor (Dharamsala, India: Library of Tibetan Works & Archives, 1979), p. 57.
2. Saint Symeon the New Theologian, quoted in *Teachings of the Christian Mystics,* ed. Andrew Harvey (Boston: Shambhala, 1998), p. 60.
3. Helena Roerich, *Heart* (New York: Agni Yoga Society, 1975), p. 272.
4. Hadewijch of Antwerp, quoted in *Teachings of the Christian Mystics,* ed. Harvey, p. 84.
5. Thurman, *Essential Tibetan Buddhism,* p. 142.
6. Ibid., p. 160.
7. Mark L. Prophet and Elizabeth Clare Prophet, *Lords of the Seven Rays: Mirror of Consciousness* (Corwin Springs, Mont.: Summit University Press, 1986), pp. 258–59.

8. Daniel C. Matt, *God and the Big Bang: Discovering Harmony between Science and Spirituality* (Woodstock, Vt.: Jewish Lights Publishing, 1996), p. 73.

9. Wolfe Lowenthal, *There Are No Secrets: Professor Cheng Man-ch'ing and His Tai Chi Chuan* (Berkeley, Calif: North Atlantic Books, 1991), pp. 111, 67.

10. Gerry Spence, *How to Argue and Win Every Time* (New York: St. Martin's Press, 1995), pp. 28–29.

Part 5   ENTERING THE HEART

1. *The Prayers of Catherine of Siena,* ed. Suzanne Noffke (New York: Paulist Press, 1983), pp. 104, 91.

2. See Elizabeth Clare Prophet with Patricia R. Spadaro, *The Art of Practical Spirituality: How to Bring More Passion, Creativity and Balance into Everyday Life* (Corwin Springs, Mont.: Summit University Press, 2000), pp. 39–52.

3. Taken from Kuthumi and Djwal Kul, *The Human Aura* (Corwin Springs, Mont.: Summit University Press, 1996), pp. 158, 159–60, 161, 162, 194.

4. Swami Prabhavananda and Christopher Isherwood, *How to Know God: The Yoga Aphorisms of Patanjali* (New York: New American Library, Mentor, 1969), pp. 49, 50.

5. Ibid., p. 49.

6. Ibid., pp. 49–50.

7. *The Way of Perfection* 28:2, 9–11, in *The Collected Works of St. Teresa of Avila,* trans. Kieran Kavanaugh and Otilio Rodriguez (Washington, D.C.:

ICS Publications, 1980), 2:140, 143–44.

8. Muggeridge, *Something Beautiful for God,* pp. 74–75.

9. Compiled from Catherine of Siena's prayers. See *The Prayers of Catherine of Siena,* ed. Noffke, pp. 105, 100, 131, 82.

10. Gabriele Uhlein, *Meditations with Hildegard of Bingen* (Santa Fe, N. Mex.: Bear & Company, 1983), pp. 94, 95–96.

11. *Lotus Prayer Book* (Yogaville, Va.: Integral Yoga Publications, 1986), p. 85.

12. Thurman, *Essential Tibetan Buddhism,* pp. 160, 161.

13. *Lotus Prayer Book,* p. 180.

Acknowledgments

We express our deep appreciation and gratitude for the wonderful team that helped nurture this book to completion, including Nigel J. Yorwerth, Louise J. Hill, Karen Gordon, Lynn Wilbert, Roger Gefvert and Virginia Wood.

For more information

Summit University Press books are available at fine bookstores worldwide and at your favorite on-line bookseller. For a free catalog of our books and products, please contact Summit University Press, PO Box 5000, Corwin Springs, MT 59030-5000 USA. Tel: 1-800-245-5445 or 406-848-9500. Fax: 1-800-221-8307 or 406-848-9555. E-mail: info@summituniversitypress.com Web site: www.summituniversitypress.com

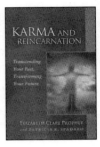
Karma and Reincarnation

Transcending Your Past,
Transforming Your Future

The word *karma* has made it into the mainstream. But not everyone understands what it really means or how to deal with it. This insightful book will help you come to grips with karmic connections from past lives that have helped create the circumstances of your life today. You'll discover how your actions in past lives—good and bad—affect which family you're born into, who you're attracted to, and why some people put you on edge. You'll learn about group karma, what we do between lives, and how to turn your karmic encounters into grand opportunities to shape the future you want.

ISBN: 0-922729-61-1
224 pages $6.95

Soul Mates and Twin Flames

The Spiritual Dimension
of Love and Relationships

"After thirty-five years as a relationship counselor, I find *Soul Mates and Twin Flames* to be extremely powerful in revealing the inner mysteries of the soul and the true essence of love through its insightful analysis of real-life experiences and classical love stories."

—MARILYN C. BARRICK, Ph.D.,
   author of *Sacred Psychology of Love*

ISBN: 0-922729-48-4
166 pages $5.95

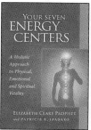

Your Seven Energy Centers
A Holistic Approach to Physical, Emotional and Spiritual Vitality

"What is so beautiful about this book is that it can speak to everyone about revitalization and inner peace."

—MAGICAL BLEND MAGAZINE

"Marries ancient healing wisdom with practical spiritual insights to help you create your own dynamic and uniquely personal healing journey. Your 21st-century guide to integrating and healing body, mind and soul."

—ANN LOUISE GITTLEMAN, author of *The Living Beauty Detox Program*

"A small book with a big message.... This handy little guide is packed with useful insights." —WHOLE LIFE TIMES

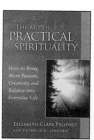

The Art of Practical Spirituality
How to Bring More Passion, Creativity and Balance into Everyday Life

Create your own intimate relationship with Spirit. This commonsense guide offers practical steps for staying in tune with Spirit midst the hustle and bustle of everyday life. For listening to the still small voice within. For living in the here and now. And it gives creative techniques we can use to uplift ourselves and the world around us.

Saint Germain On Alchemy

Formulas for Self-Transformation

"If you think alchemy is just some archaic sleight of hand for changing lead into gold, *Saint Germain On Alchemy* will set you straight. It's about transformation: transforming yourself—first spiritually and then materially. But it doesn't stop there. Alchemy aims to transform the world itself, to guide the unfoldment of history."

—RICHARD NOLLE, author of *CRITICAL ASTROLOGY*

ISBN: 0-916766-68-3
pocketbook 540 pp. $7.99

Four books in one, including *Studies in Alchemy* and *Intermediate Studies in Alchemy* plus a section on how to experience the full potential of your heart...

"Your heart is indeed one of the choicest gifts of God. Within it there is a central chamber surrounded by a forcefield of such light and protection that we call it a 'cosmic interval'.... Be content to know that God is there and that within you there is a point of contact with the Divine, a spark of fire from the Creator's own heart, called the threefold flame of life. There it burns as the triune essence of love, wisdom and power. Each acknowledgment paid daily to the flame within your heart... will produce a new sense of dimension for you."

—SAINT GERMAIN

Spiritual Techniques to Heal Body, Mind and Soul

"As we enter what Larry Dossey calls 'Era Three medicine,' programs like this one greatly enhance our lives. ...Allows a deeper connectiveness and understanding of how, in a fast-paced world, we can maintain spiritual cohesiveness. I recommend this tape for the novice, avid seeker and advanced student."

—DANNION BRINKLEY,
author of *Saved by the Light*

ISBN: 0-922729-59-X
90-min. audiocassette
$10.95

Elizabeth Clare Prophet, bestselling author and pioneer in practical spirituality, explores dynamic techniques for using the creative power of sound to transform our personal lives and bring spiritual solutions to today's global challenges.

Learn how to combine visualization, affirmation and meditation to fulfill greater levels of your own inner potential. Shows how to access a high-frequency spiritual energy to improve relationships, increase mental clarity and energize the body's seven energy centers. Includes research from well-known experts on the science of mantra.

SUMMIT UNIVERSITY ❧ PRESS®
To order call 1-800-245-5445